how2become

11+ Non-Verbal Reasoning in a Week

For the CEM (Durham University) Test

www.How2Become.com

As part of this product you have also received FREE access to online tests that will help you to pass 11+ assessments.

To gain access, simply go to:

www.MyEducationalTests.co.uk

Get more products for passing any test at:

www.How2Become.com

Orders: Please contact How2Become Ltd, Suite 3, 40 Churchill Square Business Centre, Kings Hill, Kent ME19 4YU.

You can order through Amazon.co.uk under ISBN: **9781912370313**, via the website www.How2Become.com or through Gardners.com.

ISBN: **9781912370313**

First published in 2018 by How2Become Ltd.

Typeset by Katie Noakes for How2Become Ltd.

Disclaimer

Every effort has been made to ensure that the information contained within this guide is accurate at the time of publication. How2Become Ltd is not responsible for anyone failing any part of any selection process as a result of the information contained within this guide. How2Become Ltd and their authors cannot accept any responsibility for any errors or omissions within this guide, however caused. No responsibility for loss or damage occasioned by any person acting, or refraining from action, as a result of the material in this publication can be accepted by How2Become Ltd.

The information within this guide does not represent the views of any third party service or organisation.

Contains public sector information licensed under the Open Government Licence v3.0.

CONTENTS

ABOUT THE 11+

WHAT IS THE 11+?

All across the country, Year 6 pupils will need to make that all important decision as to where they want to continue their education. Choosing the right secondary school will have a huge impact on the rest of their academic life, and thus this choice needs to be the right one for your child.

The first big decision you and your child will need to make is whether or not they wish to attend a grammar secondary school. If you wish to apply for a grammar school placement, then there are a few things that you are going to need to know.

This ultimate 11+ CEM resource will guide you through the entire process of applying to ANY grammar secondary school. This resource will answer some of the most common questions concerning the 11+ CEM, in the hopes of making the transition from primary to grammar school much, much easier.

THE NON-VERBAL REASONING TEST

Non-Verbal Reasoning questions are designed to test your ability to recognise patterns and sequences in sets of abstract shapes and pictures. There are a variety of different types of non-verbal reasoning tests which require you to pick up upon and apply a range of different methods.

Non-Verbal Reasoning is used during the 11+ so that students' ability to work out similarities of patterns and shapes can be assessed.

As mentioned previously, the Non-Verbal section of the 11+ will be combined with the verbal reasoning.

PREPARING FOR THE EXAM

The CEM 11+ is used in a number of counties throughout England, and has been designed to be 'un-tutorable'. While it may be difficult to tutor your child through the CEM 11+, it's entirely possible to learn the kinds of questions that appear in the CEM 11+, so that you aren't caught off guard by what you're faced with on the day.

The CEM 11+ is an incredibly important test for many children, since it can be the difference between attending their secondary school of choice and ending up at their second choice of school. For this reason, we believe that it is vital for children sitting the CEM 11+ to be as prepared as possible.

The CEM 11+ is made up of four main sections, which are split across two separate papers:

* Comprehension;

* Verbal Reasoning;

* Numerical Reasoning;

* Non-Verbal Reasoning.

Students sitting the CEM 11+ will sit two papers. These tend to be divided into the following sections:

PAPER 1

* Comprehension;

* Verbal Reasoning.

PAPER 2

* Numerical Reasoning;

* Non-Verbal Reasoning.

While this is the overall structure of the CEM 11+, students might find that these areas will cross over. For example, you might find a small Non-Verbal Reasoning section in paper 1.

HOW TO USE YOUR GUIDE

This guide comprises a full breakdown of the Non-Verbal Reasoning test for the CEM Durham University test.

Not only have we provided you with a rundown of what to expect, how to prepare and top tips for students and parents, but this book will be great to tailor your revision in just 7 days!

Take a look at the below structure to get an idea about how this guide will be formatted:

DAY 1

Non-Verbal Reasoning Question Type 1
Odd One Out

Non-Verbal Reasoning Question Type 2
Identical Shapes

DAY 2

Non-Verbal Reasoning Question Type 3
Find the Figure Like the Others

Non-Verbal Reasoning Question Type 4
Test Shapes

DAY 3

Non-Verbal Reasoning Question Type 5
Rotations

Non-Verbal Reasoning Question Type 6
Reflections

Non-Verbal Reasoning Question Type 7
Complete the Pair

Non-Verbal Reasoning Question Type 8
Complete the Series

Non-Verbal Reasoning Question Type 9
Complete the Grids

Non-Verbal Reasoning Question Type 10
Code Breakers

Non-Verbal Reasoning Question Type 11
3D Rotations

Non-Verbal Reasoning Question Type 12
3D Building Blocks

Non-Verbal Reasoning Question Type 13
2D Views of 3D Shapes

Non-Verbal Reasoning Question Type 14
Cubes and Nets

ADVICE FOR STUDENTS

In order for your child to score highly in their 11+, you need to ensure that they have everything they need to achieve high marks! It is important that you and your child are fully aware of what the 11+ consists of. The more familiar you are with what to expect, the better their chances will be when they sit down to take the tests.

Below is a list of GOLDEN NUGGETS that will help you AND your child to prepare for the 11+.

Golden Nugget 1 – Revision timetables

When it comes to exams, preparation is key. That is why you need to sit down with your child and come up with an efficient and well-structured revision timetable. It is important that you work with your child to assess their academic strengths and weaknesses, in order to carry out these revision sessions successfully.

TIP – Focus on their weaker areas first!

TIP – Create a weekly revision timetable to work through different subject areas.

TIP – Spend time revising with your child. Your child will benefit from your help and this is a great way for you to monitor their progress.

Golden Nugget 2 – Understanding the best way you learn

There are many different ways to revise when it comes to exams, and it all comes down to picking the way that you will find most useful.

Below is a list of the common learning styles that you may want to try:

- *Visual – the use of pictures and images to remember information;*
- *Aural – the use of sound and music to remember information;*

- *Verbal – the use of words, in both speech and writing, to understand information;*

- *Social – working together in groups;*

- *Solitary – working and studying alone.*

Popular revision techniques include: mind mapping, flash cards, making notes, drawing flow charts, and diagrams. Try as many different methods as possible to see which style you learn from the most.

TIP – Work out what kind of learner your child is. What method will they benefit from the most?

TIP – Try a couple of different learning aids and see if you notice a change in your child's ability to understand what is being taught.

Golden Nugget 3 – Break times

Allow your child plenty of breaks when revising. It's really important not to overwork your child, particularly for tests such as the 11+, which are not marked on a pass or fail basis.

TIP – Practising for 10 to 15 minutes per day will improve your child's reading ability.

Golden Nugget 4 – Practice, practice, and more practice!

Purchase past practice papers. Although the curriculum will have changed for 2018, practice papers are still a fantastic way for you to gain an idea of how your child is likely to be tested.

Golden Nugget 5 – Variety is key!

Make sure that your child learns a VARIETY of different mathematical techniques. Broadening their understanding of different techniques will help them prepare effectively for their non-verbal assessment.

TIP – Sit down with your child and go through lots of different TYPES of non-verbal reasoning questions. This way, your child will have a fuller understanding of the types of questions that they could face during their assessment.

Golden Nugget 6 – Encourage your child to discuss their work

When your child is undergoing practice questions, ask your child to talk about what they have just read. Did they understand it? Did they know what all the words meant?

TIP – Sit down with your child and ask them questions about what they have just read. Have them read a page and then test their knowledge by creating questions about the text. Have they understood everything?

Golden Nugget 7 – Stay positive!

The most important piece of preparation advice we can give you is to make sure that your child is positive and relaxed about these tests. Don't let the 11+ worry you, and certainly don't let them worry your child.

TIP – Make sure the home environment is as comfortable and relaxed as possible for your child.

Golden Nugget 8 – Answer the easier questions first

A good tip to teach your child is to answer all the questions they find easiest first. That way, they can swiftly work through the questions before attempting the questions they struggle with.

TIP – Get your child to undergo a practice paper. Tell them to fill in the answers that they find the easiest first. That way, you can spend time helping your child with the questions they find more difficult. Spend some time working through the questions they find difficult and make sure that they know how to work out the answer.

Golden Nugget 9 – Make sure they refer back to the text

One of the biggest mistakes a child can make in their Reading Comprehension SAT, is that they don't refer back to the text. All of the answers can be found in the text, therefore they should support their answers with information taken from the passage, as opposed to relying on their memory.

Golden Nugget 10 – Understanding key terms

Each assessment area has different key terms that your child needs to learn. Make sure your child spends time reading and understanding the key terms so that they increase their chances of success!

> TIP – Why not make your child's learning fun? Write down all of the key terms and cut them out individually. Do the same for the definitions. Get your child to try and match the KEY TERM with its definition. Keep playing this game until they get them all right!

ADVICE FOR PARENTS

- You may believe that the onus is really on your child's school to prepare them for their upcoming exam. While this is the case to some extent, it has been shown that parents' support and encouragement for their child to practice outside of school, can massively improve their performance.

- Do not overload your child with stacks of work. You should avoid making your child feel overwhelmed; this will only serve to discourage them. As with many things, it is best to break up their revision sessions into small, manageable chunks. This will ensure that their concentration levels remain high and they are able to take in the information that is being covered.

- Following on from the last point, make sure you schedule in plenty of rest breaks for your child. Allow them to go outside or participate in an activity that they enjoy doing. This boosts their energy and prepares them for the next time they sit down to study.

- Reward their progress and achievements. This doesn't have to mean anything extravagant, but when they have done well, or mastered a certain type of question that they had been struggling with, a small reward will make it all feel worthwhile.

- Have key notes or definitions placed around your home or your child's bedroom so that they are there to glance at every now and then. This will refresh the memory subliminally and help small portions of information to sink in. Visual aids are a great way to stimulate a child's brain.

- Encourage your child not to feel embarrassed about speaking up regarding topics they don't understand. Talking to teachers and peers will aid them during the learning process.

- Plan to focus on a specific topic in each 'session'. This will ensure that it is not too overwhelming and your child's focus is set. Begin with a topic that they find the most challenging and interchange this with a topic that they are confident on – this will keep their confidence at a stable level.

- Encourage note-taking and bullet point-making. If your child is simply reading through questions and working them out in their head, or speaking aloud the answers, it is less likely that the information will be retained than if it is written down.

- Make sure your child has an environment to study in which is as distraction free as possible. Somewhere not too noisy or cluttered will be the most productive kind of environment for them to work in. This will also mean that they will get more done, as they'll avoid potential interruptions.

- Similarly, when your child has set aside some time to revise, make sure that the television is off, there are no phones available, and the focus is purely on the subject for that period of time. This means that once it is time for a break, these things will serve as a reward for them in their free time.

- Once your child has become confident with a certain type of question, try encouraging them to practise under timed conditions. They do not necessarily have to do a whole past paper in one sitting, but even just a section whilst being timed will help to give them an idea of what it will feel like on the day of the exam.

- Gradually build up to longer sessions. If your child is having trouble concentrating, start with short twenty minute sessions and aim to build them up, over the course of their exam preparation, in small steps. This makes a lot more sense than sitting your child down for an hour or two and expecting them to stay concentrated from the outset.

- It may sound obvious, but make sure your child is getting enough sleep. If you haven't already, try and establish a solid routine. This will mean that they are able to concentrate and retain more information.

- It is especially important to try and ensure that your child gets adequate sleep the night before the exam. Try not to make them feel too stressed or pressured in the evening, and reassure them that you are confident in their abilities. This will alleviate some of the worrying that can occur in the days leading up to the exam.

- Let your child know that you are proud of them — whatever the outcome. They do not need the added pressure of worrying about potential failure. The best thing you can do is to encourage them. Avoid putting them under any added pressure.

- Getting the right nutrition is also essential for everything from concentration, to sleep, to mood. Ensure your child is eating healthily and has a well-balanced diet. Consuming too much sugar or high-fat foods will make your child's energy levels peak and then crash, and thus negatively affect their performance.

- Similarly, make sure your child is getting plenty of fresh air and exercise. They should be spending a small amount of time outside each day. This will also keep their concentration levels high and help them to sleep better every night.

- Try not to leave revision to the last minute. This will only make your child feel stressed and anxious. If you start introducing small, manageable bites of revision a good amount of time before the exam, it will make for a much more productive outcome in the long run.

In summary, we recommend positively encouraging your child, helping them to revise gradually and progressively over time. Also, it's extremely important that you constantly aim to increase their confidence. Make sure they are getting everything they need at home such as a comfortable environment to study in and a well-balanced diet, and reward them for their achievements.

We wish you and your child the best of luck in their exams!

A CHAPTER FULL OF TIPS

Not only do we think its important to learn about the structure and content of your exam, but we also think it practical that you revise some top tips and soak up some of the best exam advice prior to commencing your revision.

Tip 1 – Find out as much as you can!

Before your exam, you should find out as much information as you can about what you'll face on the day.

Below are some of the most essential things that you SHOULD know before undergoing your revision:

- The examination board;

- The subject content;

- Understanding how much each section is worth (in percentage).

Tip 2 – Create a timetable

It is important that every minute leading up to your exam is spent wisely and effectively.

The best way to do this is to create a timetable for yourself and try to adhere to it as much as possible.

On the following page, we have created a sample timetable that you can fill out according to your assessment.

	Mon	Tues	Wed	Thurs	Fri	Sat	Sun
9am – 10am							
10am – 11am							
11am – 12pm							
12pm – 1pm							
1pm – 2pm							

	Mon	Tues	Wed	Thurs	Fri	Sat	Sun
2pm – 3pm							
3pm – 4pm							
4pm – 5pm							
5pm – 6pm							
6pm – 7pm							

Tip 3 – Practise different types of questions

Sadly, revising for Non-Verbal Reasoning can be a bit of a pain. The best way to get better at Non-Verbal Reasoning assessments is to simply undergo as much practice as possible.

Another key thing to practice is timing. Chances are, you will be timed in your assessment. Therefore you want to ensure that you practice your time management.

Tip 4 – Answer practice questions

Once you're confident that you know all of the different types of non-verbal reasoning questions, it's time to get to work on practice questions. As usual, get hold of some past papers and answer all of the questions that are relevant to your course.

The most difficult part of using practice questions to revise for Non-Verbal Reasoning is that you will need to find someone to read and mark your essay, so that you know where you're doing well, and where you need to improve. Ask your teacher if it's possible for them to take a look at your answers, and they might be able to give you some pointers, giving you a rough idea of what to work on next.

Tip 5 – Read the mark scheme

Remember to use mark schemes and explanations when practising for Non-Verbal Reasoning assessments.

By going through how to reach the correct answers to every question will guarantee that you improve your knowledge next time around.

Tip 6 – Practise your handwriting

Handwriting is vital because the examiner needs to be able to read what you have written in order to mark it accurately. If the examiner can't read your work, they won't mark it. Therefore, you should spend some time practising handwriting if you think yours isn't up to standard. You'll probably be writing very quickly in the exam, which means that your handwriting will probably be less legible than usual.

Tip 7 – Always have a plan

When it comes to success at 11+, the most valuable thing is to plan. Once you open your exam paper, you might find a question that's perfect. You might be tempted to go head-first into your answer because you want to secure the marks, but it pays to exercise restraint and take the question more slowly. In fact, planning will make your time much more valuable, since you'll have a good idea of what direction your answer is going in.

Planning your answer is beneficial for two reasons. Firstly, it'll force you to look at the question more closely. This means that you'll answer the actual question in the paper, rather than misinterpret it or create a question in your head that you would like to answer. Many students fail to answer the question directly, and planning will help you clarify what's being asked of you in the exam.

Tip 8 – Pay attention to everything

Pay attention to everything! If you are unsure about what the differences are, or what is happening in the sequences, pay attention to everything you see. Count all the sides, angles, colours, shading, line types, sizing, rotations, reflections etc. That way you can eliminate what is the same and what is different about the sequence.

Tip 9 – Learn the best revision techniques for you

There are three major ways that people revise and absorb information. These are:

- **VISUAL** – This involves using visual aids such as note-taking and creative mapping of information, to commit things to memory.

- **AURAL** – The use of videos, music or other recordings to allow information to sink in.

- **KINAESTHETIC** – Using activities which involve interaction, to remember key details (such as flashcards and revision games).

Different paths will work better for different people, but also bear in mind that certain subjects will also suit these methods differently.

Essentially, you will need to experiment with different styles in order to find which ones best suit you, but you will also need to discover what works for each of your subjects.

Tip 10 – Ease into it

Before you start, revision can feel like a huge mountain, impossible to climb to the top of. It can be incredibly daunting. You might be overwhelmed by the feeling that you are completely unprepared and don't know enough. That said, you need to make a start sometime. Some revision is better than no revision at all, so if you're struggling to get started with your studies, ease your way into it. Start by revising for a much shorter period of time, and maybe focus on the things that you already know well or most enjoy. Once you're comfortable and confident, move onto something that you're less sure of.

Tip 11 – Treat yourself

Make sure you keep yourself motivated with some treats. You don't need to go overboard, but the "carrot and stick" method of revision can keep you working for longer periods of time, allowing you to get through more work. Things like "I'll get some ice cream, but only after I've done the next 3 pages" are a great way of keeping you going and keeping your spirits up.

Tip 12 – Think ahead

Finally, always think ahead past exams. Life continues after your 11+, and you'll be treated to an extra-long summer once you've finished. You might feel that you're not in a great place while revising, that your social life is suffering or your free time is being eaten up by studies, but it will all be worth it when you get great results. This positive outlook – thinking towards the future – is one of the best ways to get you started with revision, and keep you going with it too.

| Tip 13 – Use highlighters |

Using highlighters is a great way to distinguish your answers. Highlighting is helpful if you are counting lots of shapes or working out numbers or angles etc.

| Tip 14 – Visualise the question |

Try and visualise the questions!

Why not make yourself a cube net as you try to work out the cube-based questions? This will help you to visualise where the shapes on the cube will be positioned once you have folded the cube together.

Try drawing out the questions as you go. Drawing out the answers of what you think it may look like (i.e. if the shape is rotated or reflected etc), will help you to visualise the answers more clearly.

| Tip 15 – FREE testing suites! |

Check out our free online psychometric testing and sample questions to ensure that you are fully prepared for your Non-Verbal Reasoning tests.

www.MyEducationalTests.co.uk

IDENTIFYING THE NON-VERBAL REASONING PATTERN

SHAPES

When you sit a Non-Verbal Reasoning assessment, everywhere you turn you will see shapes.

In order to be competent in Non-Verbal Reasoning, you will need to familiarise yourself with shapes and have the ability to spot patterns between them.

| Sides, symmetry and rotational symmetry |

The type of shape that you see, will depend on the number of sides that it has.

TRIANGLE	NO. OF SIDES	LINES OF SYMMETRY	ROTATIONAL SYMMETRY
	• 3 sides	• 3 lines of symmetry	• Rotational symmetry of order 3

QUADRILATERAL	NO. OF SIDES	LINES OF SYMMETRY	ROTATIONAL SYMMETRY
	• 4 sides	• 4 lines of symmetry	• Rotational symmetry of order 4

PENTAGON	NO. OF SIDES	LINES OF SYMMETRY	ROTATIONAL SYMMETRY
	• 5 sides	• 5 lines of symmetry	• Rotational symmetry of order 5

HEXAGON	NO. OF SIDES	LINES OF SYMMETRY	ROTATIONAL SYMMETRY
	• 6 sides	• 6 lines of symmetry	• Rotational symmetry of order 6

HEPTAGON	NO. OF SIDES	LINES OF SYMMETRY	ROTATIONAL SYMMETRY
	• 7 sides	• 7 lines of symmetry	• Rotational symmetry of order 7

OCTAGON	NO. OF SIDES	LINES OF SYMMETRY	ROTATIONAL SYMMETRY
	• 8 sides	• 8 lines of symmetry	• Rotational symmetry of order 8

The same shape can still look different

Even though a shape may have the same number of sides, it might look different. This is because the length of the sides or angles will be different, which will make the shape look different.

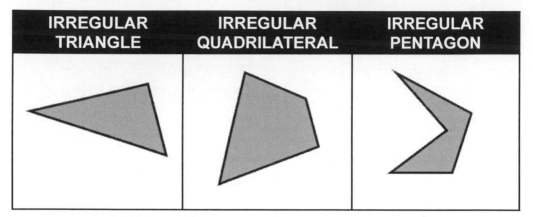

| IRREGULAR TRIANGLE | IRREGULAR QUADRILATERAL | IRREGULAR PENTAGON |

- The triangle has 3 different side lengths. Its angles would also be different.

- The quadrilateral has 4 different side lengths. Its angles would also be different.

- The pentagon has 5 different side lengths. Its angles would also be different.

Things to remember:

- Shapes have different numbers of sides. For Non-Verbal Reasoning questions, it is important that you look at what shapes are included. This might give you an insight into the pattern.

- Don't be fooled by how a shape looks. Some shapes will look different even though they have the same number of sides.

- Some questions might focus on the number of sides a shape has. For example, a sequence may be progressing by adding one side to the previous shape - i.e. three, four, five and so on.

- Don't forget to add the curved lines too. Curved lines are still classed as a side.

- Consider the size of the shape.

- Consider the symmetry of the shape.

POINTING AND COUNTING

Pay attention to the number of points

These questions are relatively straightforward, but sometimes it is tricky to count shapes without miscalculating. Be sure to pay attention and do exactly what the question is asking you.

If the question is asking you to count points, you do not need to count all of the lines, just count how many points you can see. If the question asks you to count how many sides the shape has, only count the sides of the shape.

Use a highlighter pen to highlight and count the number of points. That way you won't count the same one twice.

Counting is important

Some questions may require you to count. The sequence may be progressing by containing four black squares.

Let's take a look at an odd one out question:

In the above example, you should count the number of pentagons and the number of lines. You should notice that all but one answer figure contains the same number of lines as pentagons. That means the odd one out would be the one with two pentagons and only one line.

Things to remember:

- Use a highlighter pen to highlight and count the number of points. That way you won't count the same one twice.

- Some questions require a little working out. You will need to look for relationships between shapes. For example, a question's pattern might be that the number of dotted lines is one less than the number of sides the shape has.

- Counting everything will help you see what is changing and what stays the same in the sequence.

SHADING

Often in patterns, shapes will be shaded in a certain way. They could be white, black, grey, spotted or hatched. These are some of the most common forms of shading in Non-Verbal Reasoning questions, so we suggest that you understand how this links to the sequence.

Don't be fooled with hatching

One of the most common mistakes is that people don't pay close attention to the way the hatching is represented.

For example, take a look at the below hatched squares. Can you work out how they are different?

The hatching is going in different directions, which could be key in a question.

Horizontal hatching   Vertical hatching   Diagonal hatching going down to the right   Diagonal hatching going down to the left

Another key thing to look out for with regards to hatching is whether the line thickness is the same, whether cross-hatching is being used, or whether a different form of shading is used.

The amount of shading used

You need to pay attention to how much of the shape is shaded.

In the above examples, the figures have all been shaded exactly in half. However, the shading has been done in three different ways.

<u>Things to remember:</u>

- Work out how much of a shape is shaded. How does this pattern change throughout the sequence?

- Focus on the type of shading used. Does it use hatching? If so, what type of hatching does it use?

- You might need to add or take away shading from a figure as the sequence progresses.

- Pay attention to what shapes have been shaded. Sometimes you will be required to look at more than one shape in order to work out the sequence.

- Break down all the figures and work out the pattern for each. This will make it easier to spot patterns and sequences.

POSITIONING

Every sequence will have placed shapes in a particular place. You need to work out where a shape has been placed and how or whether this changes as the sequence progresses.

Every shape has been positioned on purpose

Some shapes may remain in the same position throughout a sequence. Some shapes may change place as the sequence progresses.

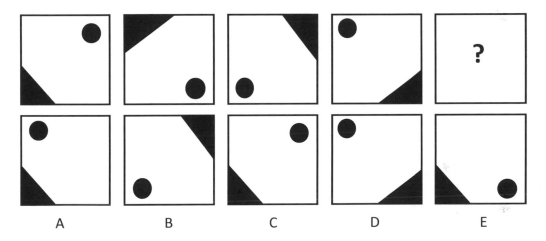

A   B   C   D   E

In the above example, you can see that the black dot moves one corner clockwise as the sequence progresses. The black triangle also moves one corner clockwise.

Based on the above sequence, the missing answer to the question would be answer option C.

The position of shapes is important

Sometimes in a sequence, shapes are added to the sequence. This means that you need to work out the new position of the shape and how this links in with the sequence.

Some shapes in a sequence might be removed. Again, you will need to work out how or where the shape is being removed from, and how the sequence progresses from there.

ROTATION

Rotation in sequences is key. Lots of Non-Verbal Reasoning questions use rotations as a way of sequence progression.

Take a look at the below example:

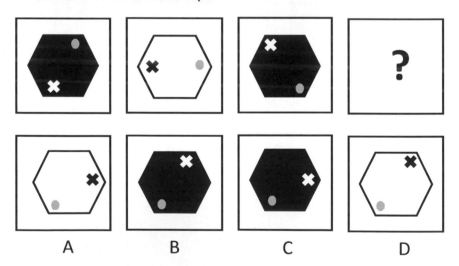

For these types of questions, you need to understand what direction the sequence has been rotated in. Not all the shapes will be rotated in the same direction, so pay attention to what is happening.

Also, you should have noticed that two different patterns are emerging; rotation and alternation. Some questions may require you to identify more than one pattern in the sequence.

Remember, if you struggle to find the pattern of a sequence, break it down! Take one shape at a time and determine what is happening to that shape as the sequence progresses. Do the same for all of the shapes until you understand everything going on in the patterned sequence.

Answer = D

- Rule 1 = the cross moves one place clockwise.

- Rule 2 = the grey dot moves one place clockwise.

- Rule 3 = you will also notice that the sequence alternates colours. The big shapes change from black to white. The cross changes from white to black. The dot remains the same colour.

REFLECTION

Reflections are another key pattern in Non-Verbal Reasoning questions.

Take a look at the below example:

 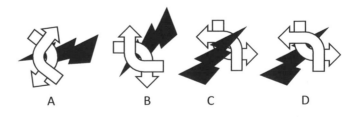

A   B   C   D

The reflections may not be seen one after another; they may be reflecting in every other box, or every third box. It is important to look closely at everything that is going on and identify the pattern and similarities of each figure.

Answer = D

Figures A, B and C are all manipulations of the shape but are not reflections. Figure D is a reflection of the Question Figure.

Reflections are relatively straightforward. You need to ensure that you know the difference between reflection and rotation. You will lose marks if you are unable to distinguish between the two.

- For these types of questions, you need to pay attention to what is being reflected.

NON-VERBAL REASONING
DAY 1

ODD ONE OUT

Odd one out questions will require you to look at a sequence and work out which figure is the odd one out. Sounds easy, right? Well, there are lots of things that you need to look out for in order to spot the difference.

Let's take a look at a quick example:

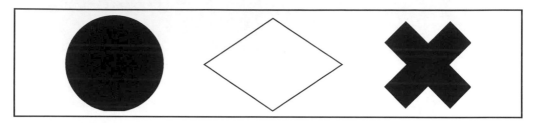

What difference can you spot?

- Two of the figures are coloured in black and only one shape is coloured in white. Therefore, the odd one out would be the white shape.

Of course, it's not always that simple when spotting the differences amongst shapes, especially when you are looking at four or five shapes in a row.

Things to remember:

- Look at each figure individually. Note down its characteristics. Do this for each figure.

- Most odd one out questions will require you to spot something that isn't always obvious at first glance.

- Sometimes, you may have to consider more than one element at a time. For example, the number of dots in the shape could be determined by the number of sides that the shape has.

Let's take a look at another example

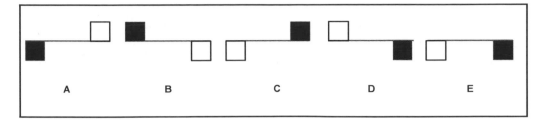

Which shape is the odd one out?

- Each figure contains two squares.

- Each figure contains a horizontal line.

- Each figure contains a black and white square.

- However, all of the figures, expect answer option E, contain one square on top of the horizontal line, and one square below the horizontal line. This is the difference and therefore makes answer option E the odd one out.

Things to remember:

Below we have outlined a list of some of the key things that you should be looking at in order to spot the difference:

- Size of shapes;

- Positioning of shapes;

- Colours of shapes;

- Shading of shapes;

- Number of shapes;

- Patterns between shapes.

DAY 1 ➡ **Odd One Out**

Example 1

Which figure is the odd one out?

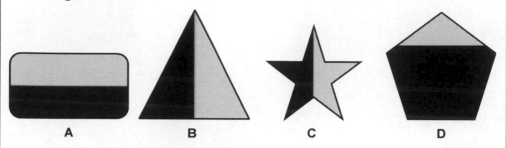

A   B   C   D

What differences can you spot?

Let's look at each figure separately and describe its characteristics:

- Figure A = rectangular shape. Half shaded in black.

- Figure B = triangular shape. Half shaded in black.

- Figure C = star shape. Half shaded in black.

- Figure D = pentagon shape. More than half shaded in black.

Therefore, the odd one out in this sequence is answer option D. This answer option has not been shaded in the same way as the other answer options.

| You need to spot what is different! |

D

Example 2

Which figure is the odd one out?

  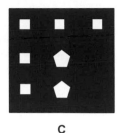 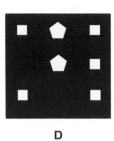

| A | B | C | D |

What differences can you spot?

Let's look at each figure separately and describe its characteristics:

- Figure A = black square. Six white squares. Two white pentagons.
- Figure B = black square. Five white squares. Two white pentagons.
- Figure C = black square. Five white squares. Two white pentagons.
- Figure D = black square. Five white squares. Two white pentagons.

Therefore, the odd one out in this sequence is answer option A. This answer option has one more white square than the other answer options.

> **Pay attention to the number of shapes each figure contains!**

A

DAY 1 → Odd One Out

Question Time!

QUESTION 1

Which figure is the odd one out?

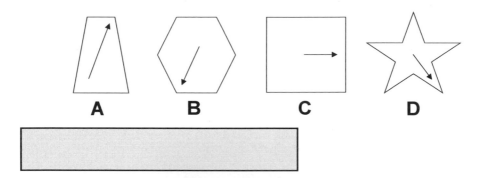

QUESTION 2

Which figure is the odd one out?

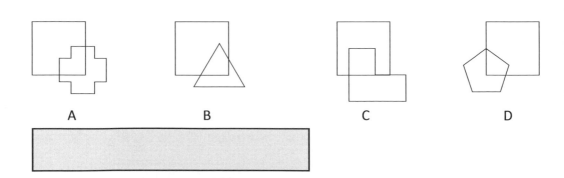

QUESTION 3

Which figure is the odd one out?

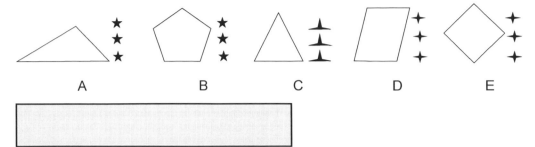

A	B	C	D	E

QUESTION 4

Which figure is the odd one out?

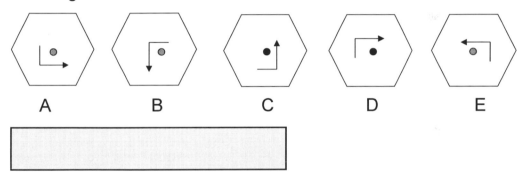

A	B	C	D	E

QUESTION 5

Which figure is the odd one out?

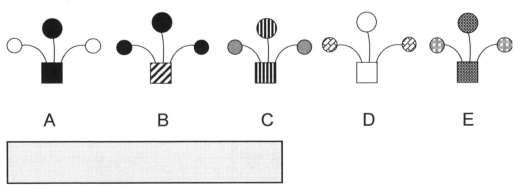

A	B	C	D	E

QUESTION 6

Which figure is the odd one out?

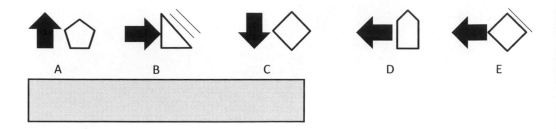

| A | B | C | D | E |

QUESTION 7

Which figure is the odd one out?

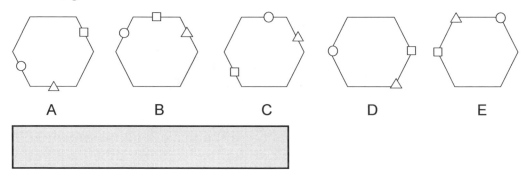

| A | B | C | D | E |

QUESTION 8

Which figure is the odd one out?

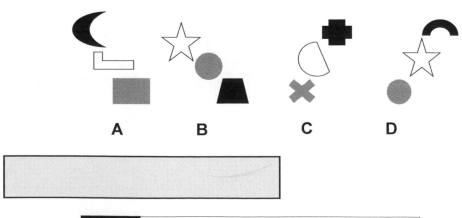

| A | B | C | D |

ANSWERS TO ODD ONE OUT

Q1. C

- Rule 1 = the arrow must point at a corner of the shape.

Figure C is the odd one out because all of the other figures contain an arrow pointing towards a corner of the large shape, whereas in Figure C, the arrow is pointing to a side, not a corner.

Q2. A

- Rule 1 = the shapes interlinked must create an inner shape that contains four sides.

Figure A is the odd one out because all of the other figures create an inner shape which contains four sides; whereas Figure A creates an inner shape that has six sides.

Q3. A

- Rule 1 = the number of points of the large shape should match the number of points on the black star-shape.

Figure A is the odd one out because the large shape contains three points, whereas the number of points on the star-shape is five.

Q4. D

- Rule 1 = Arrows move in an anti-clockwise direction.

Figure D is the odd one out. All of the other arrows are moving in an anti-clockwise direction, whereas in figure D the arrow is moving in the opposite direction.

Q5. B

- Rule 1 = the shapes opposite each other should be of the same pattern.

Figure B is the odd one out because the pattern in the square (and opposite the black circle) are not of the same colour and pattern. Either the circle should be changed to the same diagonal black and white lines, or the square should be changed to black.

Q6. C

- Rule 1 = all the sides of all the shapes in the figure, should add up to twelve.

Figure C is the odd one out because the sides of the shapes only add up to eleven.

Q7. C

- Rule 1 = working in a clockwise manner, the sequence should follow: square, triangle, circle, and then repeat.

Figure C is the odd one out because the sequence pattern is different from the other figures. Instead of following the pattern: square, triangle, circle; it follows the pattern of: square, circle, triangle.

Q8. B

- Rule 1 = a black shape should remain at the top of the figure.

Figure B is the odd one out because all of the other figures contain a black shape at the top of the figure; whereas Figure B contains a black shape at the bottom of the sequence.

IDENTICAL SHAPES

Non-Verbal Reasoning questions that require you to spot identical shapes are relatively simple. However, you need to be able to have a keen eye for detail, as the answer options will all look very similar.

> **Try not to be caught out by how similar they all look!**

Let's take a look at a quick example:

A   B   C

Which two of the above shapes are EXACTLY identical?

- In order to spot the two figures that are exactly identical, you need to spot how the other differs from them.

- As you can see, answer option A and C both contain a black dot inside the grey shape.

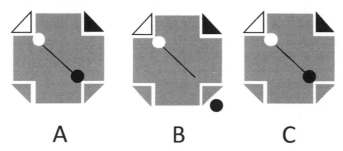

A   B   C

- Answer option B contains a black dot positioned outside of the grey shape.

- This is the only difference amongst these three shapes.

- Therefore, A and C are the identical shapes.

B

DAY 1 ➡ Identical Shapes

Things to remember:

- Look at each figure individually. Note down its characteristics. Do this for each figure.

- Most identical shapes questions will require you to spot two identical shapes.

- Sometimes, you may need to look at each element in each answer option, and see whether or not it changes.

- Try to eliminate answers. If you spot something that differs from all the other answer options, you can automatically cross this one out.

Example 1

Work out which two shapes are identical. (No rotation or reflection needed). TWO answers required.

A   B   C   D   E

- Answer option E can be ruled out because no other option contains two small arrows on the top line.

- Answer option D can be ruled out because no other option contains just one small arrow on the middle line.

- Answer option A and C are exactly identical. The reason answer option B is not identical is because, on the last line, the size of the third arrow is different.

A   C

Example 2

Work out which two shapes are identical. (No rotation or reflection needed). TWO answers required.

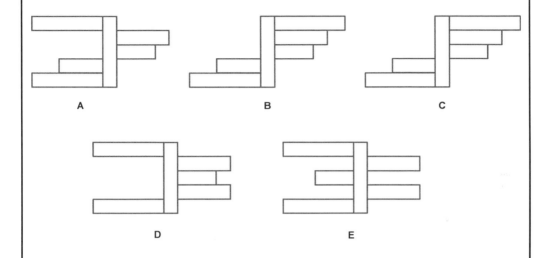

- Answer option E can be ruled out because no other option contains a horizontal rectangle in the middle on the left.

- Answer option D can be ruled out because this is the only option that doesn't contain a horizontal rectangle on the fourth line, on the left.

- Answer option A can be ruled out because no other answer option contains the top horizontal line on the right side.

- Therefore, answer option B and C are identical.

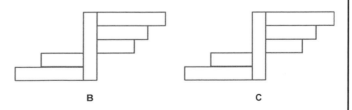

Question Time!

QUESTION 1

Work out which two shapes are identical. (No rotation or reflection needed). TWO answers required.

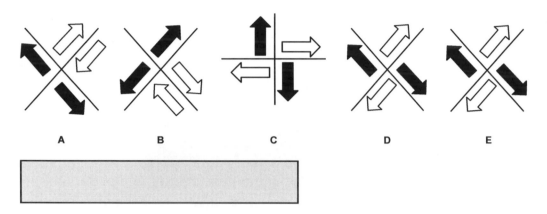

QUESTION 2

Work out which two shapes are identical. (No rotation or reflection needed). TWO answers required.

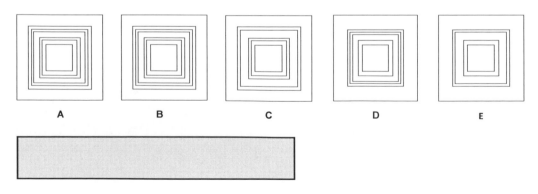

DAY 1 → **Identical Shapes**

QUESTION 3

Work out which two shapes are identical. (No rotation or reflection needed). TWO answers required.

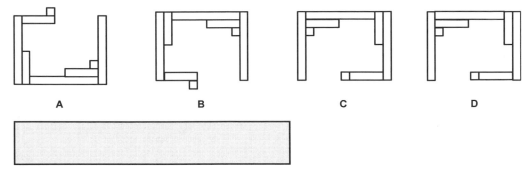

QUESTION 4

Work out which two shapes are identical. (No rotation or reflection needed). TWO answers required.

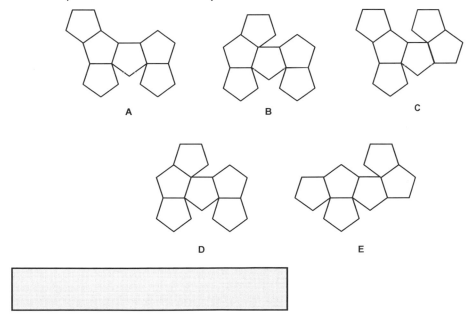

DAY 1 → **Identical Shapes**

QUESTION 5

Work out which two shapes are identical. (No rotation or reflection needed). TWO answers required.

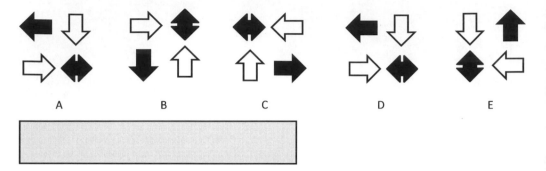

QUESTION 6

Work out which two shapes are identical. (No rotation or reflection needed). TWO answers required.

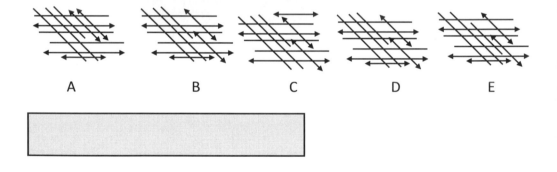

QUESTION 7

Work out which two shapes are identical. (No rotation or reflection needed). TWO answers required.

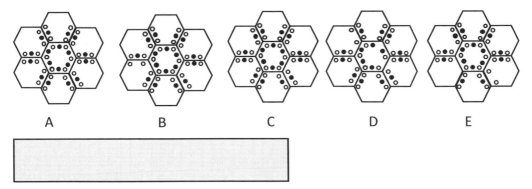

A   B   C   D   E

QUESTION 8

Work out which two shapes are identical. (No rotation or reflection needed). TWO answers required.

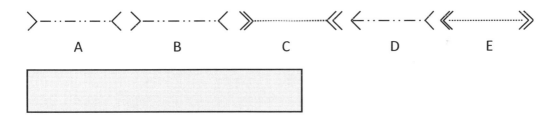

A   B   C   D   E

ANSWERS TO IDENTICAL SHAPES

Q1. D and E

- None of the other shapes are identical. Figures D and E are identical.

Q2. A and B

- None of the other shapes are identical. Figures A and B are identical.

Q3. C and D

- None of the other shapes are identical. Figures C and D are identical.

Q4. B and D

- None of the other shapes are identical. Figures B and D are identical.

Q5. A and D

- None of the other shapes are identical. Figures A and D are identical.

Q6. B and D

- None of the other shapes are identical. Figures B and D are identical.

Q7. A and C

- None of the other shapes are identical. Figures A and C are identical.

Q8. A and B

- None of the other shapes are identical. Figures A and B are identical.

Day 1 Checklist

You have now completed your Day 1 revision.

How confident are you feeling?

Below we have included a checklist that you can tick off to make sure that you have learnt everything regarding this chapter.

I have read and understood the examples for tackling Odd One Out questions. ☐

I have read and understood the examples for tackling Identical Shapes questions. ☐

I have read and understood the top tips provided for my Day 1 revision. ☐

I have read and understood the detailed answers and explanations to each question. ☐

I feel confident in Odd One Out questions. ☐

I feel confident in Identical Shapes questions. ☐

NON-VERBAL REASONING
DAY 2

FIND THE FIGURE LIKE THE OTHERS

For these types of question, you need to be able to spot the figure like the others.

Let's take a look at a quick example:

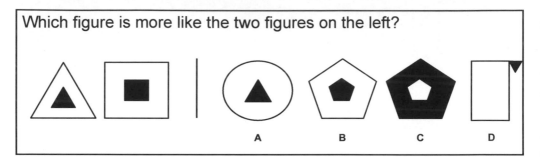

Which figure is more like the two figures on the left?

A   B   C   D

Which figure (A, B, C or D) looks like the two figures on the left?

- As you can see in the above example, the two figures on the left show a large white shape, with the same shape centred in the middle of it.

- This smaller shape is black.

- Therefore the only viable option is B.

> Find the similarities and differences between the question figures. This will help you to eliminate some answers.

Things to remember:

- Look at each figure individually. Note down its characteristics. Do this for each figure.

- Work out what the similarities and differences are amongst each of the shapes.

- Sometimes, you may have to consider more than one element at a time. For example, the number of dots in a shape could be determined by the number of sides that the shape has.

These questions require you to work out the similarities between the two figures on the left. Once you have figured out what the similarities are, you can then use them to work out the correct answer.

You need to look for the answer that demonstrates the same elements/patterns. This might not necessarily mean they will be the same shapes, so you need to ensure that you pay attention to how each figure relates to one another.

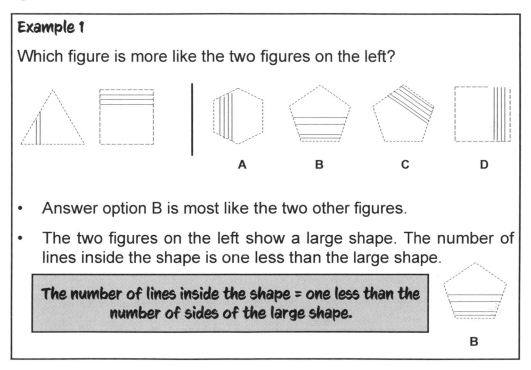

Example 1

Which figure is more like the two figures on the left?

A	B	C	D

• Answer option B is most like the two other figures.

• The two figures on the left show a large shape. The number of lines inside the shape is one less than the large shape.

> **The number of lines inside the shape = one less than the number of sides of the large shape.**

B

It's not always easy to pick out the relationship between each of the figures. Therefore, you might need to breakdown each of the shapes and see how they relate to one another.

Key things to consider:

• Number of sides

• Colour

• Symmetry

• Positioning

• Order of Rotations

• Type of Shape

DAY 2 ➡ **Find The Figure Like The Others**

Question Time!

QUESTION 1

Which figure is most like the question figures?

Question Figures

Answer Figures

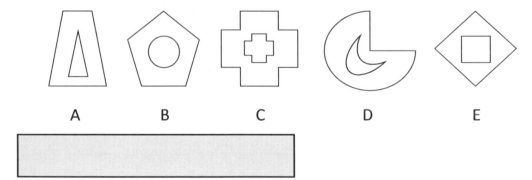

A   B   C   D   E

QUESTION 2

Which figure is most like the question figures?

Question Figures

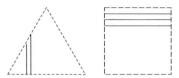

Answer Figures

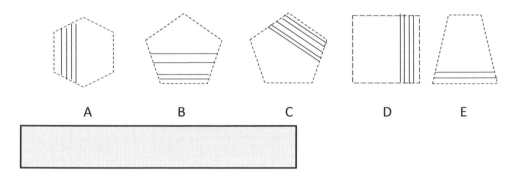

| A | B | C | D | E |

QUESTION 3

Which figure is most like the question figures?

Question Figures

Answer Figures

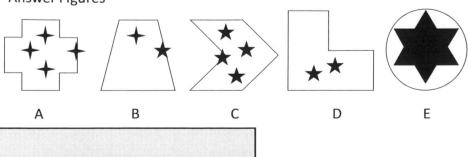

| A | B | C | D | E |

QUESTION 4

Which figure is most like the question figures?

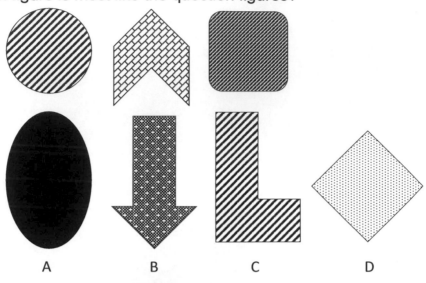

A   B   C   D

QUESTION 5

Which figure is most like the question figures?

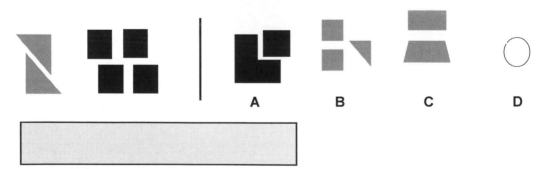

A   B   C   D

QUESTION 6

Which figure is most like the question figures?

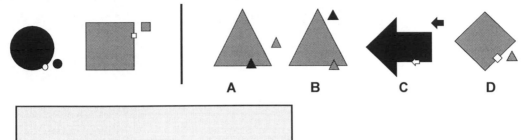

QUESTION 7

Which figure is most like the question figures?

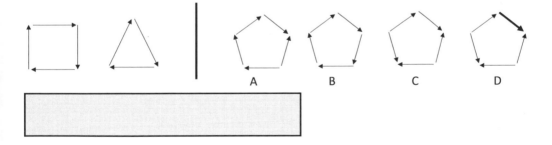

QUESTION 8

Which figure is most like the question figures?

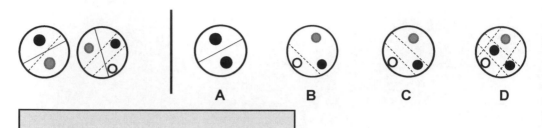

ANSWERS TO FIND THE FIGURE LIKE THE OTHERS

Q1. C

- Figure C is most like the question figures. The question figures contain a small shape inside a large shape. The small shape needs to be the same shape as the large shape.

Q2. B

- Figure B is most like the question figures. The number of lines inside the large shape is one less than the number of sides of the large shape.

Q3. C

- Figure C is most like the question figures. The question figures contain large shapes which have small, five-pointed stars. One of the five-pointed stars must be over the edge of the side of the large shape.

Q4. C

- The Question Figures all contain patterns that are diagonal (from bottom left to the top right). Figure A is completely black and therefore can be ruled out. Figure B has a grey pattern that differs from the question figures and therefore can be ruled out. Figure D has a pattern of black dots and therefore can be ruled out.

Q5. A

Answer option A is most like the two other figures. The shapes in each figure should make up a square. Only answer option A does this.

Q6. C

Answer option C is most like the two other figures. The large shape should be the same colour and shape as the small shape placed outside of this shape. The shape overlapping the side of the large shape should be white.

Q7. B

Answer option B is most like the two other figures. The two figures use pointed lines which outline a shape. The arrows all point in a clockwise direction.

Q8. D

Answer option D is most like the two other figures. A circle contains smaller circles and lines. The number of small circles is indicated by the number of lines in the large circle.

TEST SHAPE

For these types of question, you need to be able to spot the figure like the others.

Let's take a look at a quick example:

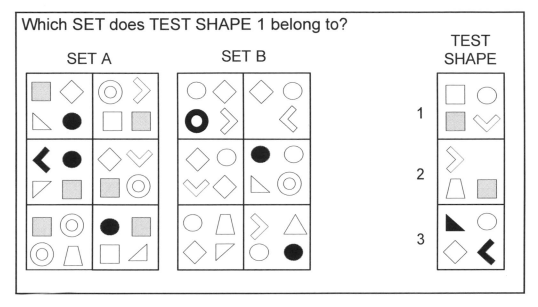

When responding to this type of question we can see that it is the 'issues around the size and shape of objects', the 'number of objects' and the 'shading and colour' that we needed to observe and assess in order to reach the correct answers.

Pay attention to what is happening in the sequence. In the above example, we are looking for links between the sets and the test shapes. Test shape 1 does not belong to either set, as it contains a shaded square and a white circle.

You will notice that neither Set A nor Set B contains a shaded square and a white circle.

In order for test shape 1 to belong to Set A, the white circle would have to change to a different shape, such as a black circle.

ANSWER = NEITHER

Example 1

Which SET does the TEST SHAPE belong to – Set A, Set B or Neither?

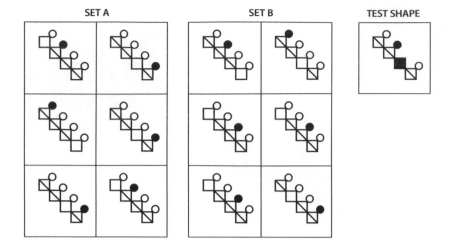

- The test shape does not belong to either of the sets.

- Set A and Set B do not contain a black square.

- Therefore the test shape cannot fit into either set.

When answering these types of question, you need to find a clear relationship between the test shape and one of the sets. If you cannot spot any connection, then the test shape will not belong to either set.

Let's take a look at another example:

Example 2

Which SET does the TEST SHAPE belong to – Set A, Set B or Neither?

SET A	SET B	TEST SHAPE

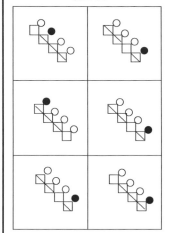 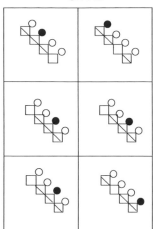

- The test shape belongs to Set B.

- In the test shape, the black dot is situated on a square with a diagonal line.

- The square beneath this will also contain a diagonal line. The square following that will be just white, and the next square in the sequence will contain a diagonal line.

Question Time!

QUESTION 1

Which TEST SHAPE belongs to SET A?

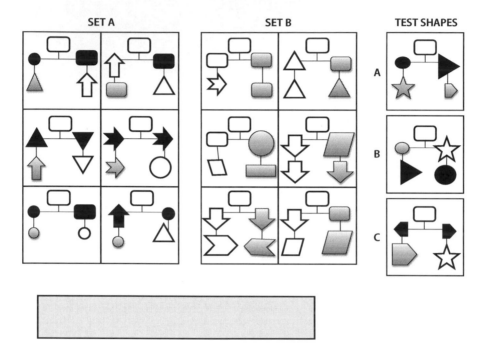

QUESTION 2

Which SET does the TEST SHAPE belong to – Set A, Set B or Neither?

SET A	SET B	TEST SHAPE

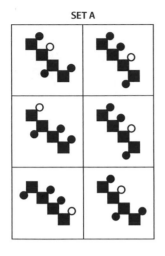 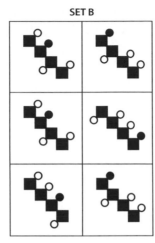

QUESTION 3

Which SET does the TEST SHAPE belong to – Set A, Set B or Neither?

SET A	SET B	TEST SHAPE

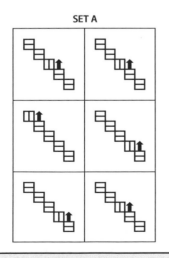 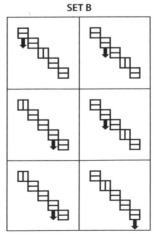 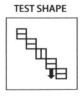

DAY 2 → **Test Shape**

QUESTION 4

Which SET does the TEST SHAPE belong to – Set A, Set B or Neither?

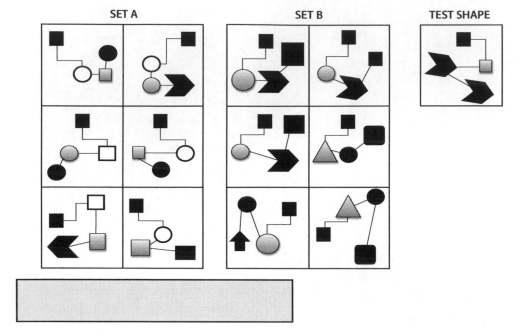

QUESTION 5

Which SET does the TEST SHAPE belong to – Set A, Set B or Neither?

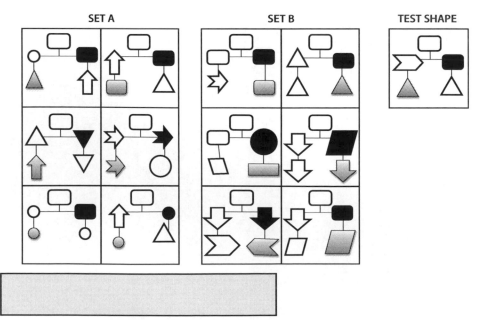

QUESTION 6

Which SET does the TEST SHAPE belong to – Set A, Set B or Neither?

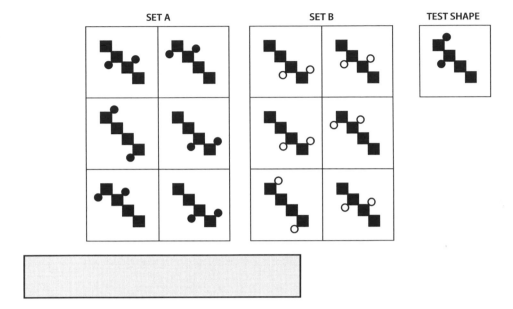

QUESTION 7

Which SET does TEST SHAPE B belong to?

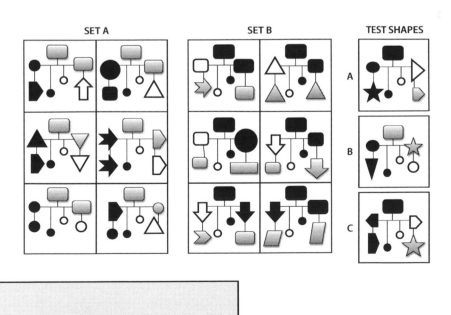

DAY 2 ➡ **Test Shape**

QUESTION 8

Which SET does the TEST SHAPE B belong to – Set A, Set B or Neither?

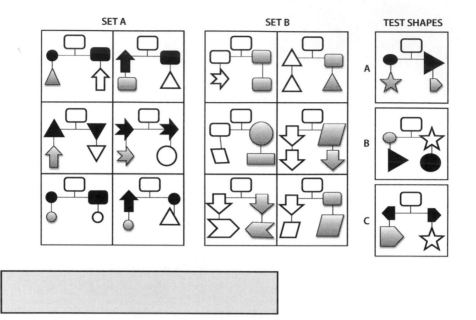

ANSWERS TO TEST SHAPE

Q1. Test Shape C

• Test Shape C belongs to Set A. It follows the exact colour pattern. The colour pattern (from top line to bottom line) is: white, black, black, grey, and white.

Q2. Neither

• The Test Shape belongs to Neither. This is because the small white circles don't fit in with either the colour scheme of Set A or Set B.

Q3. Set B

• The Test Shape belongs to Set B. In Set B, the arrow always points downwards on a square with a horizontal line.

Q4. Set B

• The Test Shape belongs to Set B. It follows the exact colour pattern. The colour pattern (from top line to bottom line) is: black, grey, white, and black.

Q5. Set A

• The Test Shape belongs to Set A. It follows the exact colour pattern. The colour pattern (from top line to bottom line) is: white, white, black, grey, and black.

DAY 2 ➡ **Test Shape**

Q6. Set A

- The Test Shape belongs to Set A. If there's no discernible pattern to either shape, then logic dictates that you would go to the next most reasonable explanation – black dots on a black line. Therefore, A is the correct answer.

Q7. Set A

- The Test Shape belongs to Set A. It follows the exact colour pattern. The colour pattern (from top line to bottom line) is: grey, black, grey, black, black, white, and white.

Q8. Neither

- The Test Shape does not follow either colour pattern, and therefore does not belong to Set A or Set B.

Day 2 Checklist

You have now completed your Day 2 revision.

How confident are you feeling?

Below we have included a checklist that you can tick off to make sure that you have learnt everything regarding this chapter.

I have read and understood the examples for tackling Find the Figures Like the Others questions.

I have read and understood the examples for tackling Test Shape questions.

I have read and understood the top tips provided for my Day 2 revision.

I have read and understood the detailed answers and explanations to each question.

I feel confident in Find The Figures Like the Others questions.

I feel confident in Test Shape questions.

NON-VERBAL REASONING
DAY 3

ROTATIONS

Rotation questions will require you to look at a sequence and work out which figure has been rotated. Sounds easy, right? Well, there are lots of things that you need to look out for in order to spot the rotations.

Let's take a look at a quick example:

Work out which option (A, B, C or D) would NOT look like the Question Figure if it was rotated.

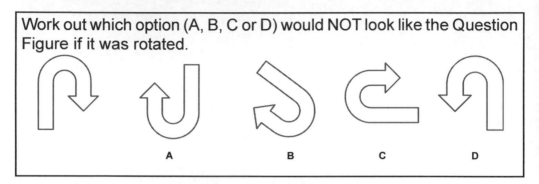

| | A | | B | | C | | D |

ANSWER = D

These types of questions require you to pay close attention to detail. You need to determine what the question is asking you.

For example, this question is asking you which figure is NOT a rotation of the Question Figure.

Therefore, you need to find which shape will not look like the Question Figure if it were to be rotated. Maybe the shape has changed slightly or maybe it is a reflection and not a rotation.

> Draw out the Question Figure on a piece of paper. Rotating the paper, you will see what answers match up.

Example 1

Work out which option (A, B, C or D) would NOT look like the Question Figure if it was rotated.

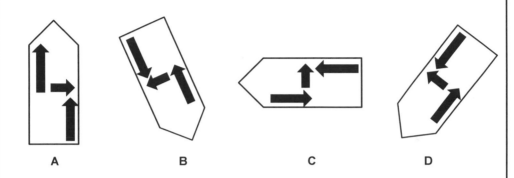

| A | B | C | D |

- The arrow at the top of the Question Figure is in the incorrect position in Figure A.

- In Figure A, the arrow is pointing in the opposite direction.

TOP TIPS!

- Make sure that you read the question carefully.

- Look at Example 1 again. Can you see that the word "NOT" changes the whole question entirely. Make sure you read the question word for word before writing your answer.

- Remember the difference between rotation and reflection. Just because something has been rotated in the same way, doesn't mean smaller shapes have stayed the same. Be sure to look out for manipulations or reflections.

DAY 3 ➡ **Rotations**

Question Time!

QUESTION 1

Which of the Answer figures is a rotation of the Question figure?

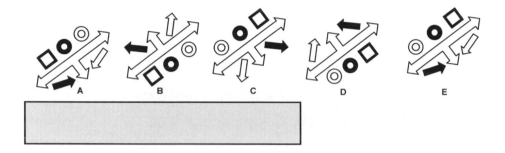

QUESTION 2

Work out which option (A, B, C or D) would NOT look like the Question Figure if it were rotated.

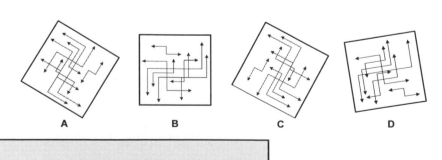

QUESTION 3

Work out which option (A, B, C or D) would NOT look like the Question Figure if it were rotated.

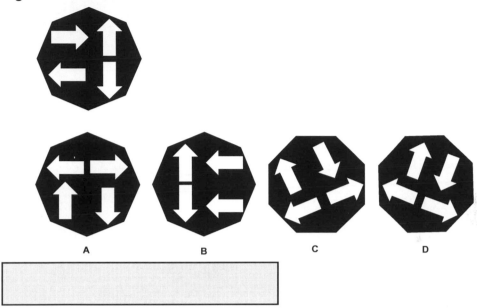

QUESTION 4

Work out which option (A, B, C or D) would NOT look like the Question Figure if it were rotated.

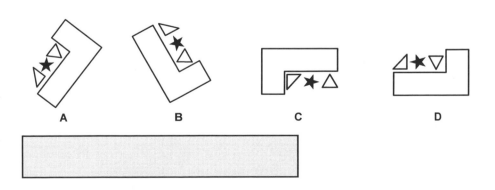

QUESTION 5

Work out which option (A, B, C or D) would NOT look like the Question Figure if it were rotated.

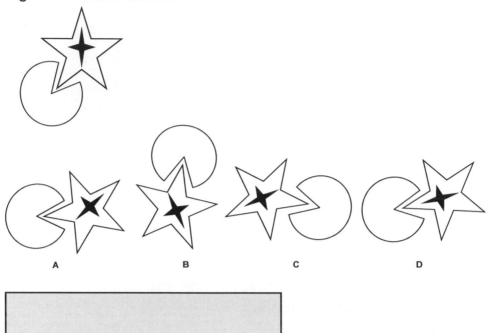

A   B   C   D

QUESTION 6

Work out which option (A, B, C or D) would NOT look like the Question Figure if it were rotated.

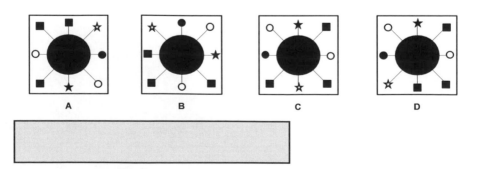

A   B   C   D

QUESTION 7

Work out which option (A, B, C or D) would NOT look like the Question Figure if it were rotated.

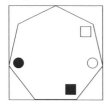

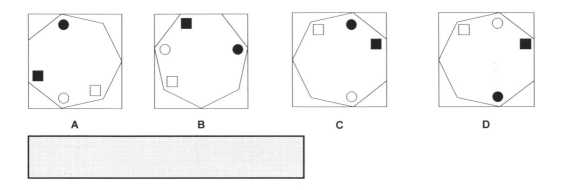

A   B   C   D

QUESTION 8

Work out which option (A, B, C or D) would NOT look like the Question Figure if it were rotated.

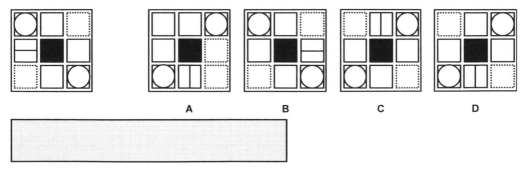

A   B   C   D

ANSWERS TO ROTATIONS

Q1. E

- Only answer option E would be a rotation of the Question Figure.

Q2. D

- Only answer option D would NOT be a rotation of the Question Figure.

Q3. B

- Only answer option B would NOT be a rotation of the Question Figure.

Q4. C

- Only answer option C would NOT be a rotation of the Question Figure.

Q5. D

- Only answer option D would NOT be a rotation of the Question Figure.

Q6. C

- Only answer option C would NOT be a rotation of the Question Figure.

Q7. C

- Only answer option C would NOT be a rotation of the Question Figure.

Q8. A

- Only answer option A would NOT be a rotation of the Question Figure.

REFLECTIONS

Reflection questions will require you to look at a figure and work out which answer options are or are not reflections. Sounds easy, right? Well, there are lots of things that you need to look out for in order to spot the difference.

Let's take a look at a quick example:

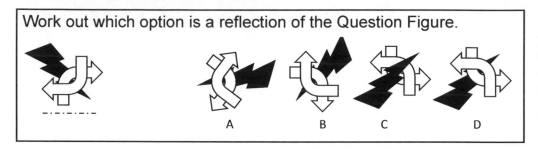

Work out which option is a reflection of the Question Figure.

A   B   C   D

ANSWER = D

Figures A, B and C are all manipulations of the shape but are not reflections. Figure D is a reflection of the Question Figure.

Reflections are relatively straightforward. You need to ensure that you know the difference between reflection and rotation. You will lose marks if you are unable to distinguish between the two.

> make sure to pay attention to where the mirror line is.

Example 1

Work out which option is a reflection of the Question Figure.

A   B   C   D

- Figures A and B are rotations, not reflections.

- Figure D is a reflection apart from the white circle being on the wrong side of the square (it should be on the bottom left side of the square, not the bottom right).

- Figure C is a reflection of the Question Figure.

ANSWER = C

Things to remember:

- For these types of questions, you need to pay attention to what is being reflected.

- These types of question can be tricky because the answer options will look very similar.

- To work through these questions quicker, you will probably be able to elminate some of the answer choices.

Question Time!

QUESTION 1

Work out which option is a reflection of the Question Figure.

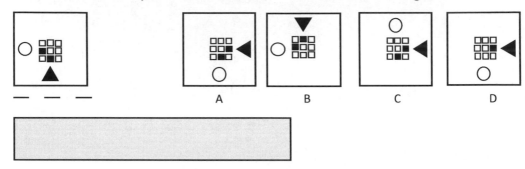

— — —

QUESTION 2

Work out which option is a reflection of the Question Figure.

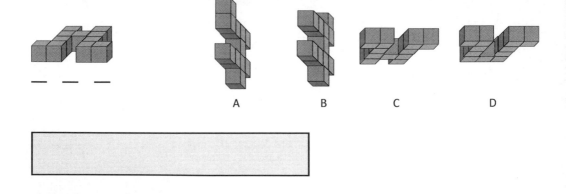

— — —

QUESTION 3

Work out which option is a reflection of the Question Figure.

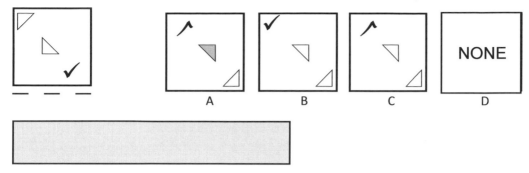

QUESTION 4

Work out which option is a reflection of the Question Figure.

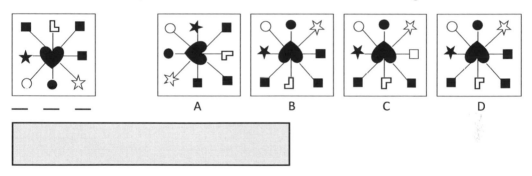

QUESTION 5

Work out which option is a reflection of the Question Figure.

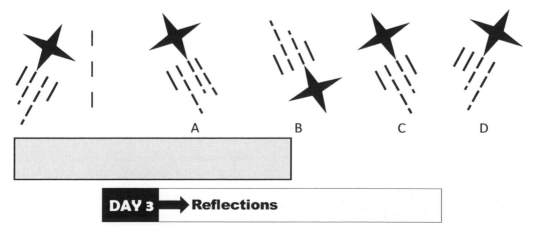

QUESTION 6

Work out which option is a reflection of the Question Figure.

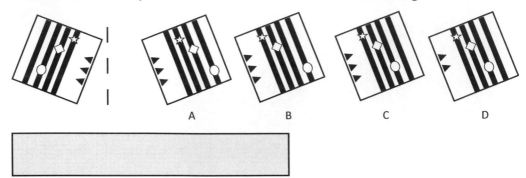

QUESTION 7

Work out which option is a reflection of the Question Figure.

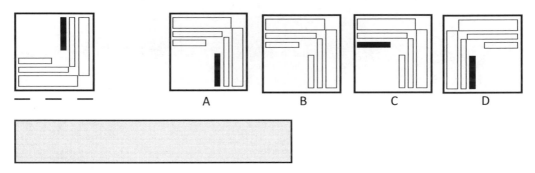

QUESTION 8

Work out which option is a reflection of the Question Figure.

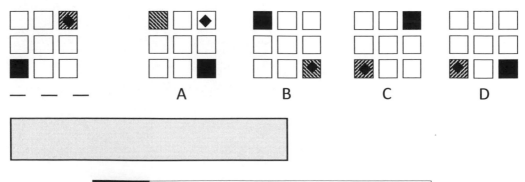

ANSWERS TO REFLECTIONS

Q1. B

- Only answer option B would be a reflection of the Question Figure.

Q2. C

- Only answer option C would be a reflection of the Question Figure.

Q3. D

- None of the answer options would be a reflection of the Question Figure.

Q4. D

- Only answer option D would be a reflection of the Question Figure.

Q5. C

- Only answer option C would be a reflection of the Question Figure.

DAY 3 ➡ **Reflections**

Q6. C

- Only answer option C would be a reflection of the Question Figure.

Q7. A

- Only answer option A would be a reflection of the Question Figure.

Q8. B

- Only answer option B would be a reflection of the Question Figure.

Day 3 Checklist

You have now completed your Day 3 revision.

How confident are you feeling?

Below we have included a checklist that you can tick off to make sure that you have learnt everything regarding this chapter.

I have read and understood the examples for tackling Rotations questions. ☐

I have read and understood the examples for tackling Reflections questions. ☐

I have read and understood the top tips provided for my Day 3 revision. ☐

I have read and understood the detailed answers and explanations to each question. ☐

I feel confident in Rotations questions. ☐

I feel confident in Reflections questions. ☐

NON-VERBAL REASONING
DAY 4

COMPLETE THE PAIR

Complete the pair questions will require you to look at a pair and work out which answer figure completes the pair underneath, using the same rules. Sounds easy, right? Well, there are lots of things that you need to look out for in order to complete the pair.

<u>Let's take a look at a quick example:</u>

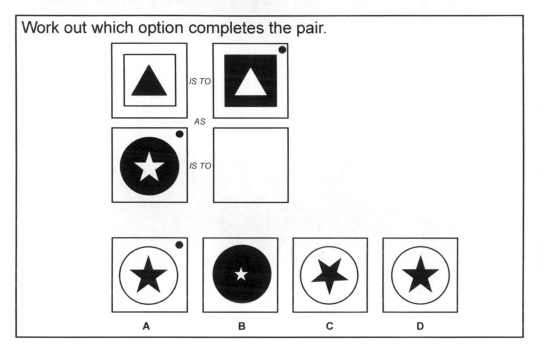

ANSWER = D

In the top left square, there is a white square with a black triangle inside. This changes to a black square with a white triangle. There is also a black dot in the top right corner.

So in the next sequence, the black circle with a white star will change to a white circle with a black star. The black dot in the top right corner will have disappeared.

Example 1

Work out which option completes the pair.

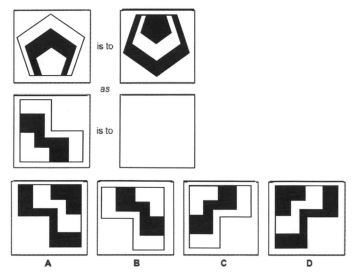

- The shape is horizontally mirrored.

- The colour pattern from white, black, and white changes to black, white and black.

ANSWER = D

Things to remember:

- Pay attention to the top row of figures. Work out how the sequence changes.

- Use that pattern to work out the missing figure in the bottom row.

Question Time!

QUESTION 1

Complete the pair.

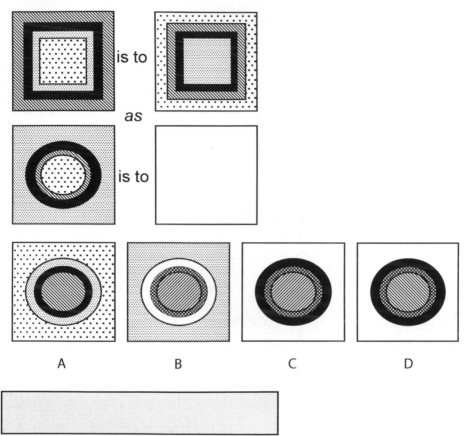

A   B   C   D

QUESTION 2

Complete the pair.

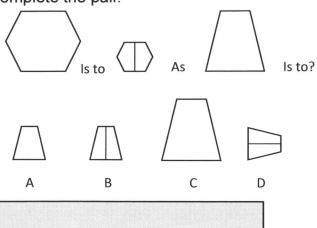

A   B   C   D

QUESTION 3

Complete the pair.

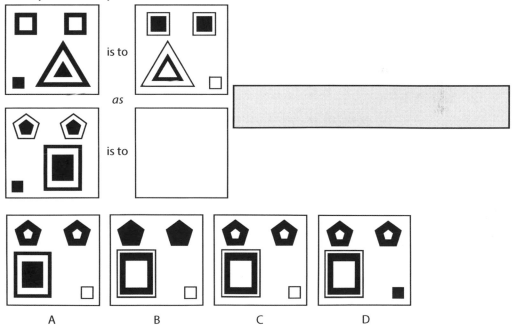

A   B   C   D

QUESTION 4

Complete the pair.

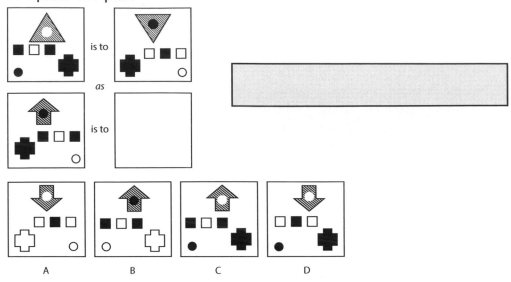

QUESTION 5

Complete the pair.

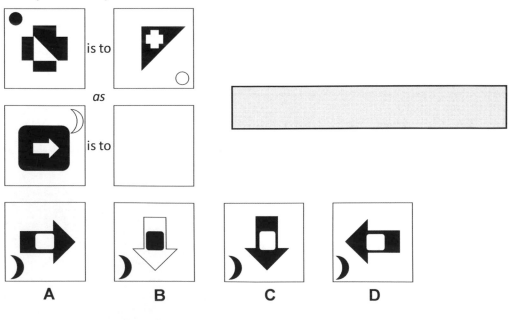

DAY 4 ➡ Complete the Pair

QUESTION 6

Complete the pair.

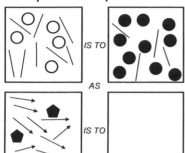

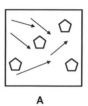

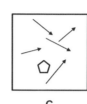

A   B   C   D

QUESTION 7

Complete the pair.

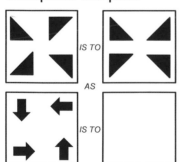

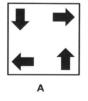

A   B   C   D

QUESTION 8

Complete the pair.

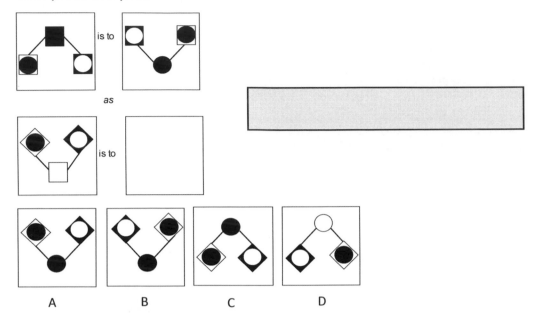

ANSWERS TO COMPLETE THE PAIR

Q1. A

- The sequence changes by the colour pattern moving inwards once each time. Therefore the colour in the centre of the circle will become the colour of the background.

Q2. B

- The large shape shrinks in size and a vertical line is added through the centre of the shape.

Q3. C

- The figure on the left is vertically reflected. The colour pattern changes. Everything that was black becomes white, and everything that was white becomes black.

Q4. D

- The arrow should become a downward pointing arrow with a white dot inside. The cross shape remains the same colour but is moved to the other side. The white dot moves to the other side and becomes black. The colour pattern changes in the three squares from black, white, black, to white, black, white.

Q5. C

- The white moon becomes black and is positioned in the corner diagonal to it. The white arrow rotates 90 degrees. The black rectangular shape is placed inside the arrow. The arrow and rectangle also invert colours.

Q6. A

- Within the first set of squares the circles double in number from 5 to 10 and change from white to black. The number of straight lines halves from 8 to 4.

Q7. A

- Within the top set of squares, the top left and bottom right shapes remain in the same position. The bottom left and top right shapes rotate 180 degrees.

Q8. D

- The central square will change to a circle, as in the first pair. This shape will stay the same colour. The central shape will move to the top as it moved to the bottom in the first pair. The other two shapes will switch shading as in the pair above.

COMPLETE THE SERIES

Complete the series questions will require you to look at a sequence and work out which figure complete the pattern. Sounds easy, right? Well, there are lots of things that you need to look out for in order to spot the difference.

Let's take a look at a quick example:

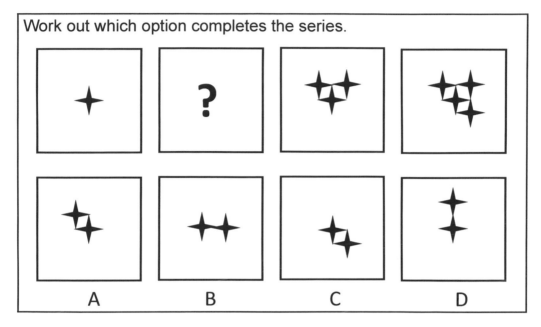

Answer = A

Rule 1 = the sequence adds one diamond each time. The diamond is added from the top left and then continues to be added in a clockwise manner.

In this example, you need to pay particular attention to numbers. The sequence follows the pattern of adding the same shape as the sequence progresses.

In other similar questions, you may need to add or subtract certain numbers of shapes in order for the sequence to be completed.

Example 1

Work out which option completes the series.

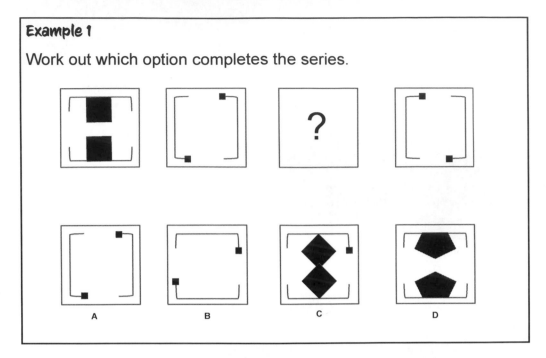

ANSWER = D

You need to pay close attention to how the sequence is progressing.

In the above example, you will notice that every even box (2 and 4) follows the same patterns, the squares alternate place on the end of the lines. Box 1 and box 3 need to be following the same pattern, it contains a black shape, inside open brackets. The answer also shouldn't have a small black square, which is why C isn't correct.

> Pay attention to small details such as positioning, shapes, colours, numbers, rotations and symmetry.

Therefore, the answer needs to contain a black shape, inside open brackets.

Question Time!

QUESTION 1

Work out which option completes the series.

 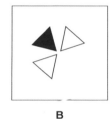  

A	B	C	D

DAY 4 ➡ **Complete the Series**

QUESTION 2

Work out which option completes the series.

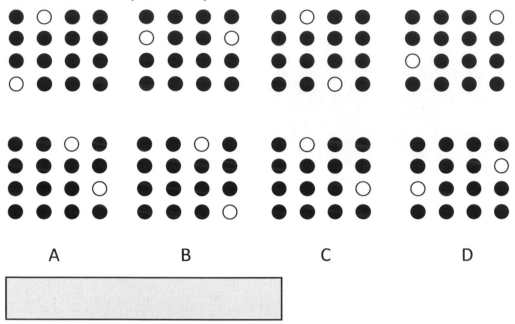

A   B   C   D

QUESTION 3

Work out which option completes the series.

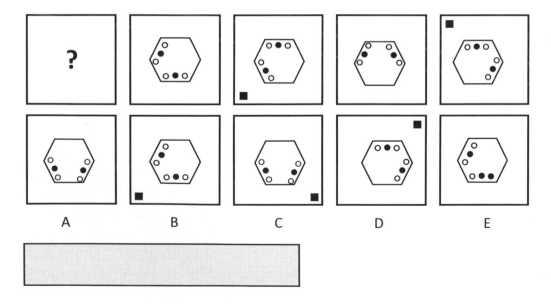

A   B   C   D   E

QUESTION 4

Work out which option completes the series.

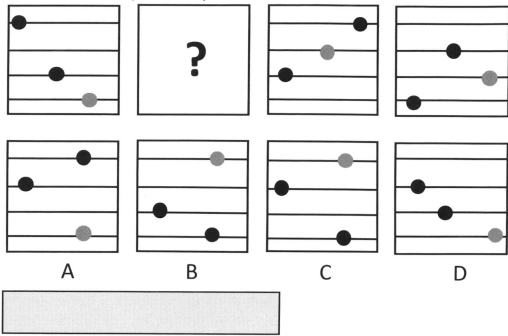

QUESTION 5

Work out which option completes the series.

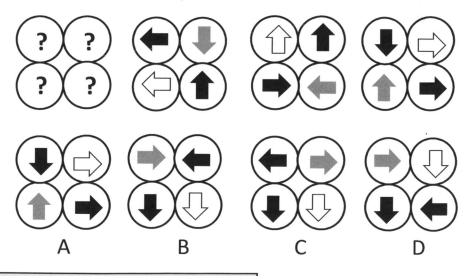

DAY 4 ➡ **Complete the Series**

QUESTION 6

Work out which option comes next in the series.

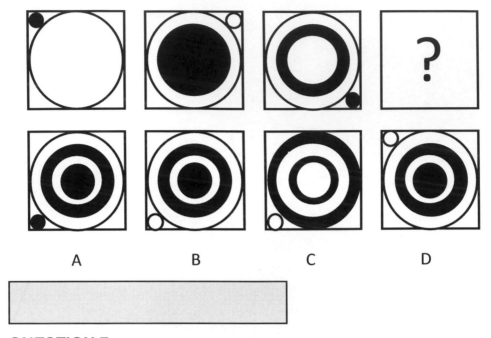

QUESTION 7

Work out which option comes next in the series.

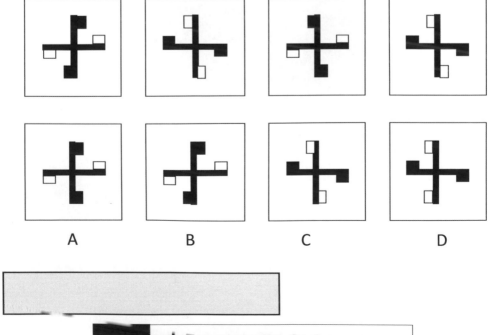

DAY 4 ➡ Complete the Series

QUESTION 8

Work out which option comes next in the series.

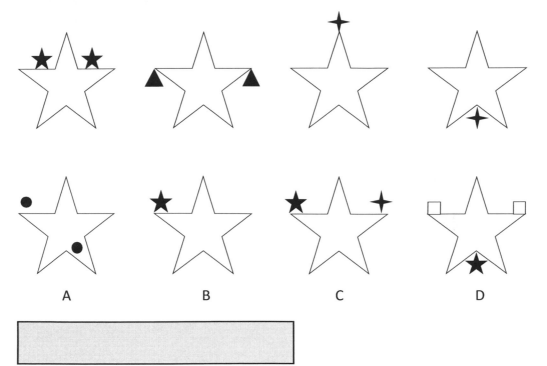

| A | B | C | D |

ANSWERS TO COMPLETE THE SERIES

Q1. A

- The triangles move round one place anticlockwise. A new white triangle is added to the end.

Q2. C

- This explanation is working backwards from the right hand box towards the left hand box. Starting from the white dot in the top right corner, this moves two spaces clockwise around the outer edge. The dot on the third row moves three spaces clockwise around the outer edge.

Q3. C

- The dots in the hexagon move around one side as the sequence progresses. In the first box in the series, a black square needs to be positioned in the bottom right corner.

Q4. C

- The dots move down one line as the sequence progresses. Once it reaches the bottom line, it makes its way back to the top line. The dots do not have to appear in the exact same place, so long as it is on the correct line.

Q5. B

- In order to work out the first in the series, the shapes need to be rotated 90 degrees anti-clockwise.

Q6. B

- As the series goes on, a smaller circle appears in the middle of the existing circle with the opposite shading. As well as this, the small circle in the corner moves around the square clockwise once each time. It also changes shading each time it moves a place. Therefore, shape b) is the correct answer. The circle in the middle of the larger shape is black and the smaller circle in the corner moves clockwise one place and changes to white.

Q7. B

- As the sequence progresses, the figures rotate 90 degrees clockwise (or anti-clockwise).

Q8. D

- The next in the series would be answer option D. To follow the pattern, the answer option needs to contain a line of symmetry.

Day 4 Checklist

You have now completed your Day 4 revision.

How confident are you feeling?

Below we have included a checklist that you can tick off to make sure that you have learnt everything regarding this chapter.

I have read and understood the examples for tackling Complete the Pair questions.

I have read and understood the examples for tackling Complete the Series questions.

I have read and understood the top tips provided for my Day 4 revision.

I have read and understood the detailed answers and explanations to each question.

I feel confident in Complete the Pair questions.

I feel confident in Complete the Series questions.

NON-VERBAL REASONING
DAY 5

COMPLETE THE GRIDS

Complete the grid questions will require you to look at a grid sequence and work out which figure is missing. Sounds easy, right? Well, there are lots of things that you need to look out for in order to complete the grids.

Let's take a look at a quick example:

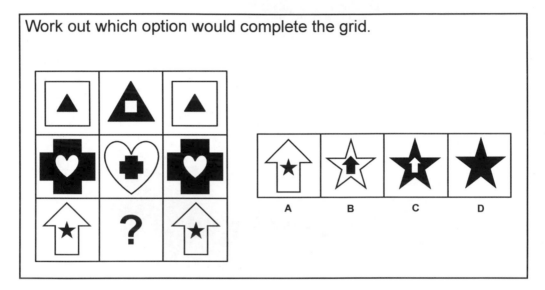

ANSWER = C

The sequence is as follows: the middle column takes the shapes from the first column and swaps them around. For example, box 1 contains a triangle inside a square that turns into a square inside a triangle.

The colour pattern changes from white on the outside and black on the inside, to black on the outside and white on the inside and vice versa. Therefore, the missing box needs to contain a white arrow inside a black star.

Example 1

Work out which option would complete the grid.

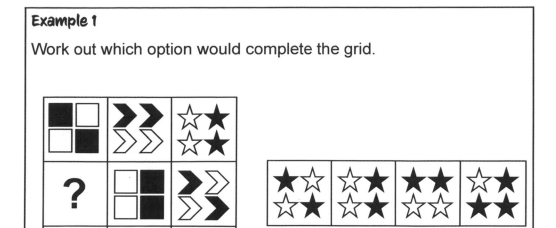

ANSWER = C

The sequence is as follows: four of the same shape in a grid format.

In each row, this sequence moves the colour pattern along, and so the diagonal colours, will now be in the middle box on the second row, and will be in the third box on the third row. Also, the shapes change (and move along one space each time): squares, chevrons, and stars.

DAY 5 ➡ **Complete the Grids**

Question Time!

QUESTION 1

Work out which option completes the grid.

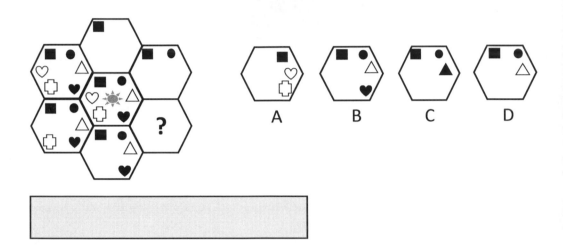

QUESTION 2

Work out which option completes the grid.

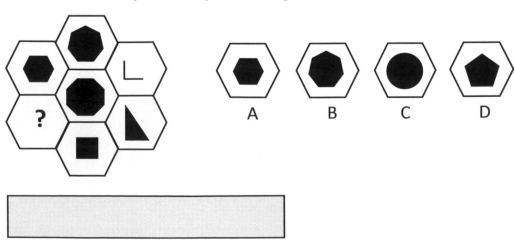

QUESTION 3

Work out which option completes the grid.

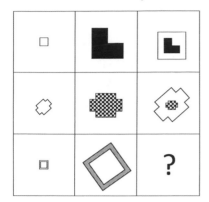

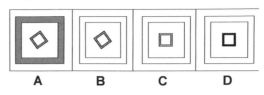

QUESTION 4

Work out which option completes the grid.

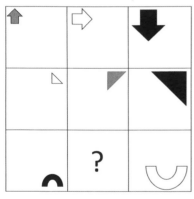

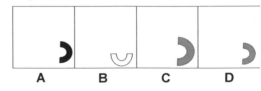

DAY 5 ➡ **Complete the Grids**

QUESTION 5

Work out which option completes the grid.

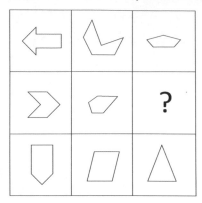

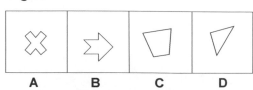

A   B   C   D

QUESTION 6

Work out which option completes the grid.

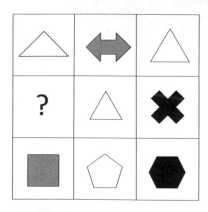

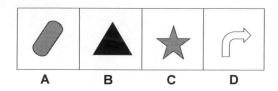

A   B   C   D

QUESTION 7

Work out which option completes the grid.

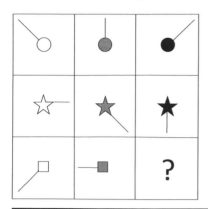

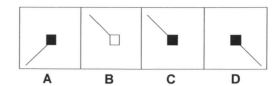

QUESTION 8

Work out which option completes the grid.

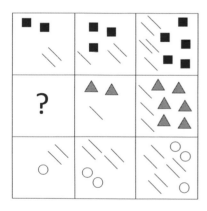

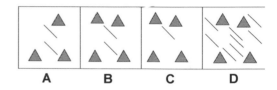

ANSWERS TO COMPLETE THE GRIDS

Q1. D

- In the grid, one shape is added in a clockwise manner. In the previous hexagon, it contains a black square and a circle. In the hexagon after the missing one it contains a black square, a black circle, white triangle, and a black square. Therefore the missing shape should contain a black square, a black circle, and a white triangle.

Q2. C

- Starting from the hexagon in the 1 o'clock position, and moving round clockwise, we can see that the number of sides is increased by one each time. Therefore the missing figure should be a five-sided shape. The pattern does not start from the top hexagon, it starts from the hexagon in the 1 o'clock position.

Q3. A

- The small shape becomes the large shape. The shape in the middle row becomes the small shape and is positioned inside the large shape.

Q4. C

- As the sequence progresses, the shapes stay in the same corner but are rotated 90 degrees clockwise. It also changes colour pattern from grey, white to black. The size slightly increases each time.

- Therefore the missing figure should be a grey arch slightly larger than the first.

Q5. C

- As the column progresses, the number of sides for each shape reduces by 1 each time. Therefore the missing figure should contain four sides.

Q6. A

- The missing figure needs to contain two lines of symmetry. From left to right, the sequence progresses by adding one more line of symmetry.

Q7. C

- The colour pattern follows: white, grey and black. The same shape appears throughout the row. The straight line moves 45 degrees clockwise each time.

Q8. B

- The number of straight lines in the first two boxes adds up to the total number of straight lines in the third box, and the same for the shapes.

CODE BREAKERS

This type of queston is rare, but is handy to learn anyhow. Learning how to break the code of a non-verbal reasoning pattern will guarantee to improve your non-verbal skills.

Let's take a look at a quick example:

Work out the codes for the figures and decide which answer has the correct code for figure 4.

1	2	3	4
D	I	D	?
Q	N	N	?

A	B	C	D
I	I	I	D
N	D	Q	Q

ANSWER = C (I, Q)

For this type of question, you will need to work out what the codes are telling you in boxes 1, 2 and 3, in order for you to work out the code for box 4.

This type of question requires a great deal of precision and understanding regarding what the code is referring to.

> Break down the codes. If a code is written twice you will be able to work out what it is referring to, based on the two shapes.

For the sample question above, you will notice that figures 1 and 3 both contain a rectangle. These rectangles are different colours, but the same size. This means that the code 'D' must represent the shape of a rectangle. You will notice that box 2 and 3 are of the same colour, but not the same shape.

However, both have a code of 'N'. This code must represent the colour. Therefore, to work out box 4, you need to find the code for both the shape and the colour. You already know that the shape of rectangles is coded 'D'. So, the code for the 'L' shape must be 'I'. (Box 2 has the code 'I' and 'N' and you have already worked out that 'N' is the code for the colour). Now you need to work out the colour. Box 1 has the same colour, and because you already know that code 'D' represents the rectangle shape, it leaves the code 'Q'.

Example 1

Work out the codes for the figures and decide which answer has the correct code for Figure 4.

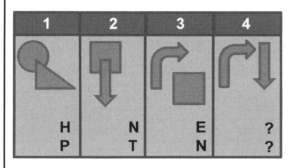

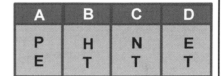

ANSWER = D

- 2 and 3 both contain squares, they also both use the code 'N' so the code for a square must be 'N'

- The other shape in 2 is a downward arrow, the other code in 2 is 'T' so the code for a downward arrow must be 'T'

- The other shape in 3 is a right-hand arrow, the other code in 3 is 'E' so the code for a right hand arrow must be 'E'

- Therefore, the code for a right hand arrow and downward arrow must be 'E T'

Question Time!

QUESTION 1

Work out the codes for the figures and decide which answer has the correct code for Figure 4.

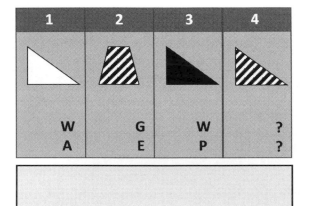

	A	B	C	D
	W	G	W	G
	A	A	E	P

QUESTION 2

Work out the codes for the figures and decide which answer has the correct code for Figure 4.

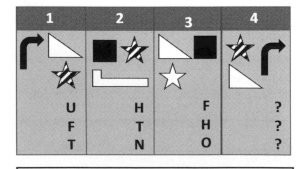

	A	B	C	D
	T	U	H	T
	U	F	O	O
	F	N	T	N

QUESTION 3

Work out the codes for the figures and decide which answer has the correct code for Figure 4.

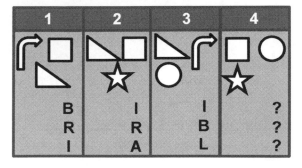

QUESTION 4

Work out the codes for the figures and decide which answer has the correct code for Figure 4.

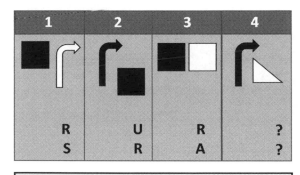

QUESTION 5

Work out the codes for the figures and decide which answer has the correct code for Figure 4.

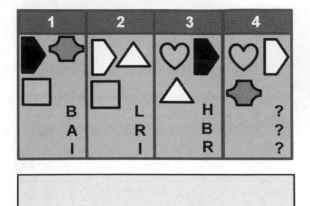

	A	B	C	D
	L	H	H	H
	O	B	O	L
	I	A	I	A

QUESTION 6

Work out the codes for the figures and decide which answer has the correct code for Figure 4.

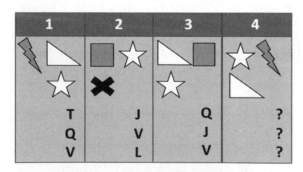

	A	B	C	D
	V	B	J	J
	T	T	B	B
	Q	Q	L	V

QUESTION 7

Work out the codes for the figures and decide which answer has the correct code for Figure 4.

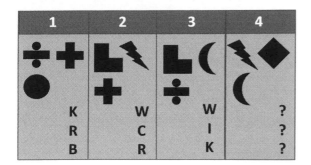

	A	B	C	D
	C	W	C	C
	R	I	A	B
	I	K	I	K

QUESTION 8

Work out the codes for the figures and decide which answer has the correct code for Figure 4.

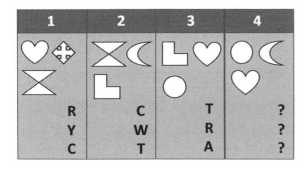

	A	B	C	D
	A	R	A	W
	R	W	W	A
	W	A	R	R

ANSWERS TO CODE BREAKERS

Q1. C

- 1 and 3 both contain triangle shapes. They also both use the code letter 'W'.

- Shape 2 has code 'G' to represent the trapezium so the code for the stripes is 'E'.

- Therefore the code for a triangle with stripy lines is 'W E'.

Q2. A

- 1 and 2 both contain stars with diagonal lines. They also both use the code letter 'T'.

- 1 and 3 both contain white triangles. They also both use the code letter 'F'.

- The black arrow is only in box 1 and the only code left is 'U' which doesn't appear in any other boxes. This must be the code for the black arrow.

- Therefore the code for a star with diagonal lines, a black arrow, and a white triangle must be 'T U F'.

Q3. B

- 1, 2 and 3 all contain white triangles. They also all use the code letter 'I'.

- 1 and 3 contain an arrow. They also both use the code letter 'B'.

- 1 and 2 contain a square. They also both contain the code letter 'R'.

- 3 contains a circle. This is the only box to use code letter 'L'.

- 2 contains a star. This is the only box to use code letter 'A'

- Therefore the code for a square, a circle, and a star would be 'R', 'L' and 'A'.

Q4. A

- 1, 2, and 3 all contain a black square. They also all use the code letter 'R'

- From this it is easy to work out that 'S' is the code for the white arrow in 1. 'U' is the code for the black arrow in 2. 'A' is the code for the square in 3.

- None of the boxes (1, 2 or 3) have a white triangle. So a code letter is needed that hasn't appeared already. In this case, the code letter 'E' represents the triangle.

- Therefore the code for a black square and a white triangle must be 'U E

Q5. D

- 1 and 3 contain a black five-sided shape. They also both use the code letter 'B'.

- 1 and 2 contain a grey square. They also both use the code letter 'I'.

- 2 and 3 contain a white triangle. They also both use the code letter 'R'.

- 1 only has code letter 'A' unaccounted for so this is the code for the grey 8 sided shape.

- 2 only has code letter 'L' unaccounted for so this is the code for the white 5 sided shape.

- 3 only has code letter 'H' unaccounted for so this is the code for the heart.

- Therefore the code for a heart, a white 5 sided shape, and a grey 8 sided shape must be 'H L A'

Q6. A

- 1, 2, and 3 all contain a white star. They also all use the code letter 'V'

- 1 and 3 both contain a triangle. They both use the code letter 'Q'.

- 1 contains a lightning bolt. The only code left is 'T', so this must be the code for the lightning bolt.

- Therefore the code for a star, a lightening bolt, and a triangle must be 'V T Q'

DAY 5 ➤ **Code Breakers**

Q7. C

- 1 and 2 both contain a plus sign. They also both use the code 'R'.

- 2 and 3 both contain an L shape. They also both use the code 'W'

- 1 and 3 both contain a divide sign. They also both use the code 'K'

- From here it is easy to work out that 'B' is the code for the circle in 1, 'C' is the code for the lightening bolt in 2, and 'I' is the code for the moon in 3.

- The diamond in 4 isn't used anywhere else so it must have a new code.

- Therefore the code for a lightening bolt, a diamond, and a moon i 'C A I'.

Q8. C

- 1 and 2 both contain shape with two triangles. They also both use the code 'C'

- 2 and 3 both contain an L shape. They also both use the code 'T'

- 1 and 3 contain a heart. They also both use the code 'R'.

- The circle in 3 must use the leftover code 'A'.

- Therefore the code for a circle, a moon, and a heart is 'A W R'

Day 5 Checklist

You have now completed your Day 5 revision.

How confident are you feeling?

Below we have included a checklist that you can tick off to make sure that you have learnt everything regarding this chapter.

I have read and understood the examples for tackling Complete the Grids questions.

I have read and understood the examples for tackling Code Breakers questions.

I have read and understood the top tips provided for my Day 5 revision.

I have read and understood the detailed answers and explanations to each question.

I feel confident in Complete the Grids questions.

I feel confident in Code Breakers questions.

NON-VERBAL REASONING
DAY 6

3D ROTATIONS

3D rotation questions will require you to look at a sequence and work out which 3D figure has been rotated.

Let's take a look at a quick example:

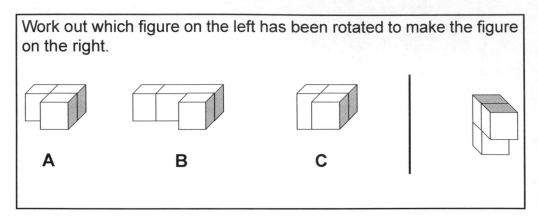

Work out which figure on the left has been rotated to make the figure on the right.

A   B   C

ANSWER = A

In the figure on the right, you can see three identical cubes.

Figure B cannot have been rotated because it contains one long cuboid. Figure C cannot have been rotated because it contains one long cuboid.

Therefore the correct answer is A.

Question Time!

QUESTION 1

Work out which figure on the left has been rotated to make the figure on the right.

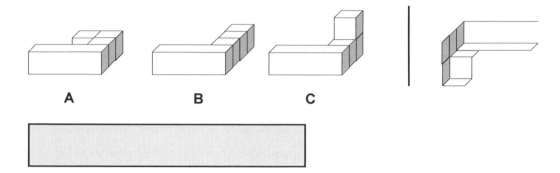

QUESTION 2

Work out which figure on the left has been rotated to make the figure on the right.

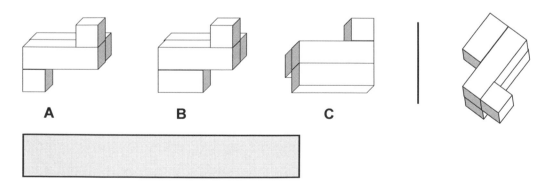

QUESTION 3

Work out which figure on the left has been rotated to make the figure on the right.

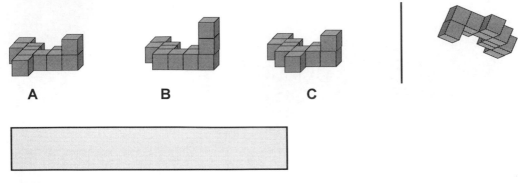

A   B   C

QUESTION 4

Work out which figure on the left has been rotated to make the figure on the right.

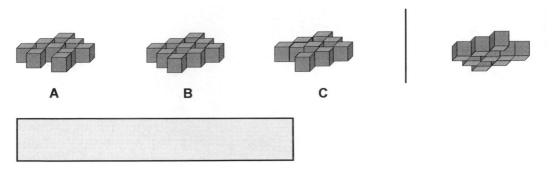

A   B   C

QUESTION 5

Work out which figure on the left has been rotated to make the figure on the right.

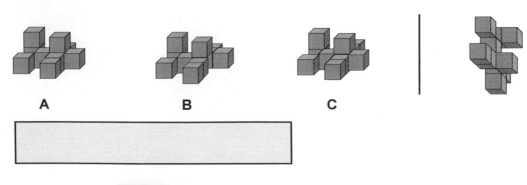

A   B   C

DAY 6 ➡ **3D Rotations**

QUESTION 6

Work out which figure on the left has been rotated to make the figure on the right.

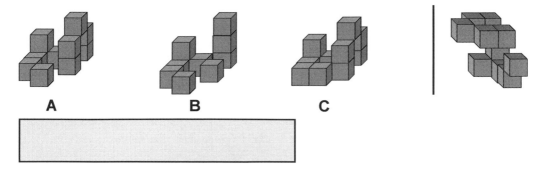

A   B   C

QUESTION 7

Work out which figure on the left has been rotated to make the figure on the right.

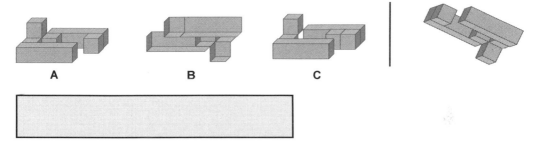

A   B   C

QUESTION 8

Work out which figure on the left has been rotated to make the figure on the right.

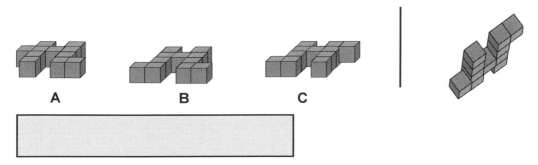

A   B   C

ANSWERS TO 3D ROTATIONS

Q1. C

- If you rotated the figure on the right, the only option that you would get is C.

Q2. B

- If you rotated the figure on the right, the only option that you would get is B.

Q3. C

- If you rotated the figure on the right, the only option that you would get is C.

Q4. C

- If you rotated the figure on the right, the only option that you would get is C.

Q5. B

- If you rotated the figure on the right, the only option that you would get is B.

Q6. A

- If you rotated the figure on the right, the only option that you would get is A.

Q7. A

- If you rotated the figure on the right, the only option that you would get is A.

Q8. C

- If you rotated the figure on the right, the only option that you would get is C.

3D BUILDING BLOCKS

For these types of question, you need to be able to visualise 3D shapes.

Let's take a look at a quick example:

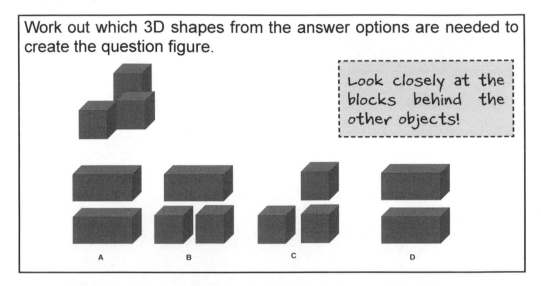

Work out which 3D shapes from the answer options are needed to create the question figure.

Look closely at the blocks behind the other objects!

A   B   C   D

ANSWER = B

For this type of question, you need to pay close attention to the Question Figure. You need to be able to identify what shapes are used to make up this particular configuration of blocks.

For such questions, blocks will be placed alongside, behind, on top, or in front of one another, in order to make the question more challenging. In this case, you can see that there are two cubes at the front.

Try drawing out the blocks. How many blocks would you need? What sizes are they? Place the blocks in different positions to see where they would fit.

The fact that the furthest back object is taller than the other cubes suggests it may be a cuboid. So, based on the answer options, you need to work out which answer it will be. The only answer that would work would be answer B.

Example 1

Work out which 3D shapes from the answer options are needed to create the question figure.

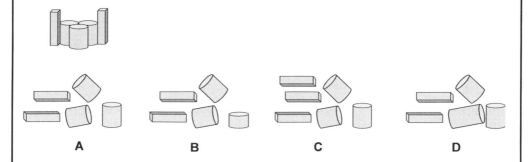

A	B	C	D

- Answer option A is the correct option.

- The question figure contains three identical cylinders, and two long cuboids.

ANSWER = A

Things to remember:

- Try drawing out the blocks. How many blocks would you need? What sizes are they? Place the blocks in different positions to see where they would fit.

- For such questions, blocks will be placed alongside, behind, on top, or in front of one another, in order to make the question more challenging. In this case, you can see that there are two cubes at the front.

DAY 6 ➡ **3D Building Blocks**

Question Time!

QUESTION 1

Work out which 3D shapes from the answer options are needed to create the question figure.

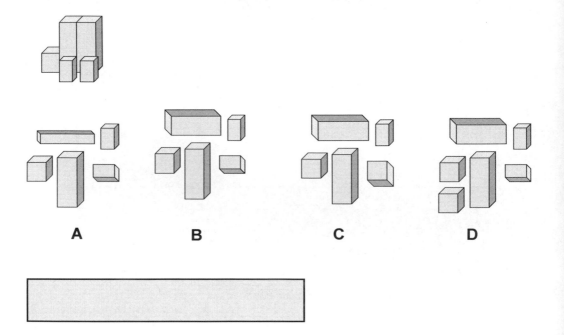

A   B   C   D

QUESTION 2

Work out which 3D shapes from the answer options are needed to create the question figure.

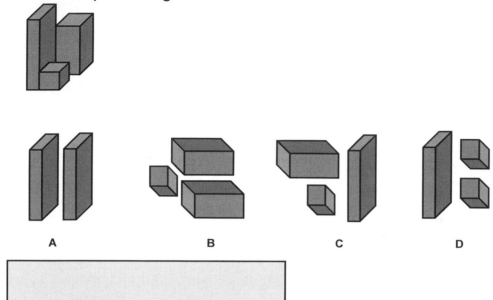

A B C D

QUESTION 3

Work out which 3D shapes from the answer options are needed to create the question figure.

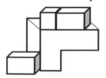

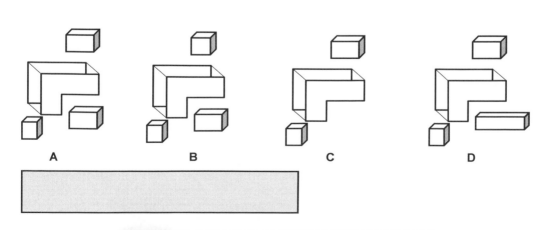

A B C D

DAY 6 → **3D Building Blocks**

QUESTION 4

Work out which 3D shapes from the answer options are needed to create the question figure.

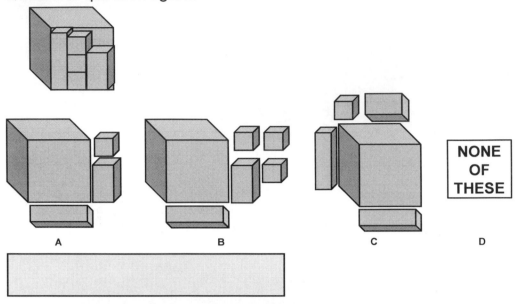

QUESTION 5

Work out which 3D shapes from the answer options are needed to create the question figure.

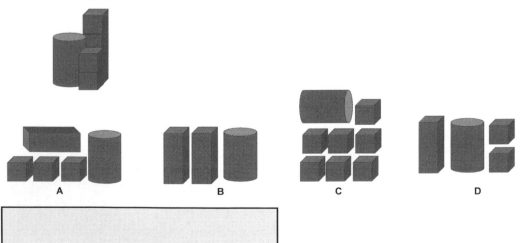

QUESTION 6

Work out which 3D shapes from the answer options are needed to create the question figure.

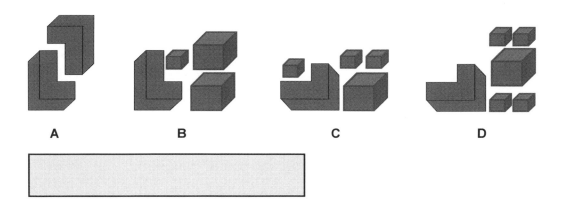

| A | B | C | D |

QUESTION 7

Work out which 3D shapes from the answer options are needed to create the question figure.

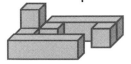

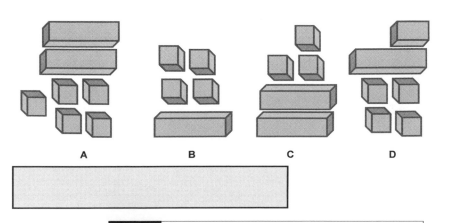

| A | B | C | D |

DAY 6 ➡ **3D Building Blocks**

QUESTION 8

Work out which 3D shapes from the answer options are needed to create the question figure.

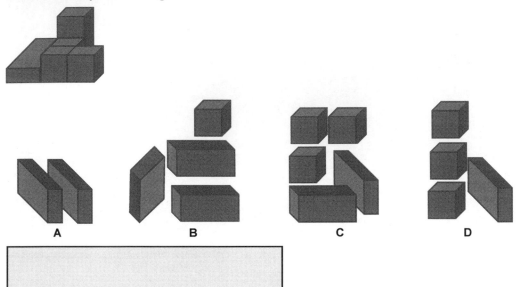

ANSWERS TO 3D BUILDING BLOCKS

Q1. B

- Answer option B is the correct option. The question figure contains one cube, two long cuboids, and two short cuboids.

Q2. C

- Answer option C is the correct option. The question figure contains one thin, long cuboid, one chunkier cuboid, and one cube.

Q3. A

- Answer option A is the correct option. The question figure contains an L-shape and two cuboids of the same size.

Q4. B

- Answer option B is the correct option. The question figure contains one large cube, one thin, long cuboid, a chunkier shorter cuboid, and three small cubes.

Q5. A

- Answer option A is the correct option. The question figure contains a cylinder, three cubes, and one long cuboid.

DAY 6 ➡ **3D Building Blocks**

Q6. D

- Answer option D is the correct option. The question figure contains an L-shaped figure, one large cuboid, and four small cubes.

Q7. A

- Answer option A is the correct option. The question figure contains five cubes and two long cuboids.

Q8. C

- Answer option C is the correct option. The question figure contains three cubes, one long thin cuboid, and one chunkier cuboid.

Day 6 Checklist

You have now completed your Day 6 revision.

How confident are you feeling?

Below we have included a checklist that you can tick off to make sure that you have learnt everything regarding this chapter.

I have read and understood the examples for tackling 3D Figures questions.

I have read and understood the examples for tackling 3D Building Blocks questions.

I have read and understood the top tips provided for my Day 6 revision.

I have read and understood the detailed answers and explanations to each question.

I feel confident in 3D Figures questions.

I feel confident in 3D Building Blocks questions.

NON-VERBAL REASONING
DAY 7

2D VIEWS OF 3D SHAPES

For these types of question, you need to be able to recognise 2D views of 3D shapes.

Let's take a look at a quick example:

Work out which figure is a top-down 2D view of the 3D question figure.

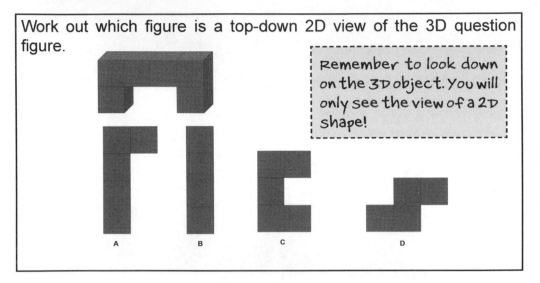

Remember to look down on the 3D object. You will only see the view of a 2D shape!

A   B   C   D

ANSWER = B

In this type of question, you have to decide which 2D figure (A, B, C or D) can be seen if you were to look at the 3D shape from a top-down point of view. **Remember to look down on the 3D object.**

The key thing to remember about this type of question is positioning. If you do not look at the 3D object in the correct way, you will struggle to get the correct answer.

Take the sample question above, you will notice the top of the 3D shape. This is the part that you need to pay attention to. This is the part that you will see from a top-down point of view.

Imagine you are a bird overlooking everything from above. What would you see? You would only see the top of everything!

Example 1

Work out which figure is a top-down 2D view of the 3D question figure.

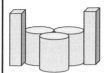

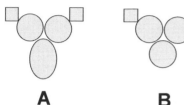 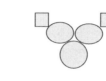 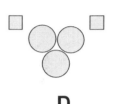

    A   **B**   **C**   **D**

- From a top down view, you would see two squares and three circles.

- These would all appear to be connected.

ANSWER = B

Things to remember:

- Imagine you are a bird overlooking everything from above. What would you see? You would only see the top of everything!

- The key thing to remember about this type of question is positioning. If you do not look at the 3D object in the correct way, you will struggle to get the correct answer.

Question Time!

QUESTION 1

Work out which figure is a top-down 2D view of the 3D question figure.

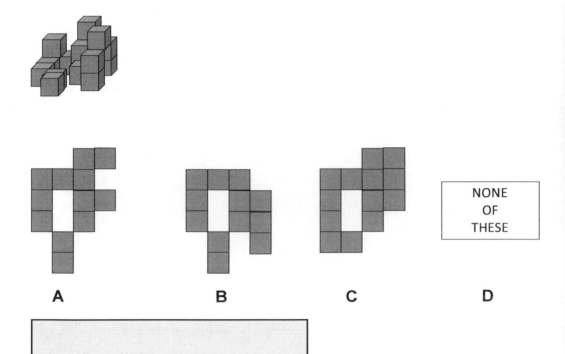

NONE
OF
THESE

A   B   C   D

QUESTION 2

Work out which figure is a top-down 2D view of the 3D question figure.

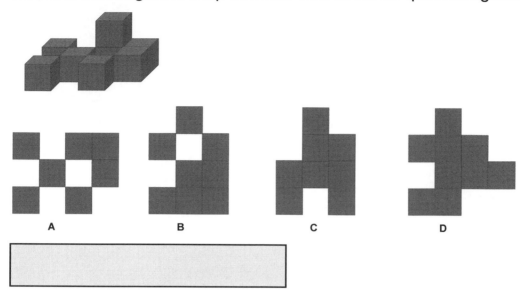

QUESTION 3

Work out which figure is a top-down 2D view of the 3D question figure.

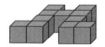

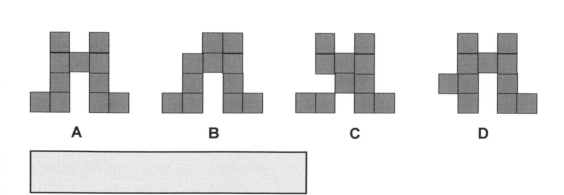

QUESTION 4

Work out which figure is a top-down 2D view of the 3D question figure.

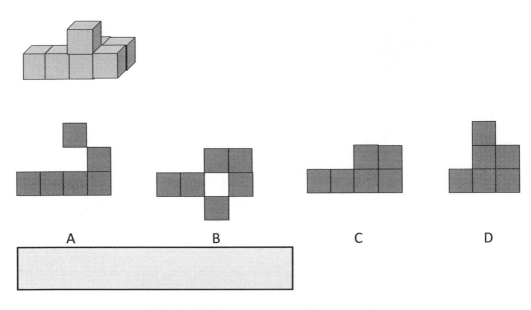

A   B   C   D

QUESTION 5

Work out which figure is a top-down 2D view of the 3D question figure.

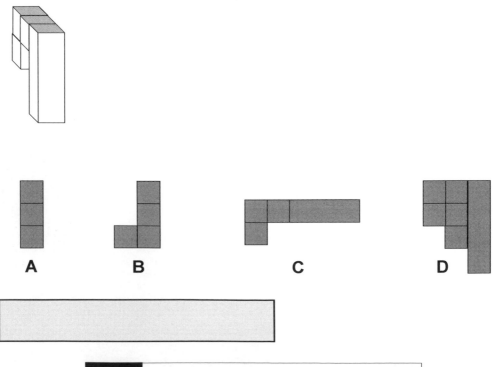

A   B   C   D

QUESTION 6

Work out which figure is a top-down 2D view of the 3D question figure.

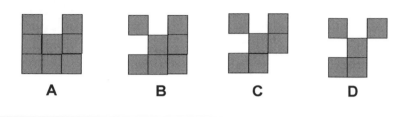

A   B   C   D

QUESTION 7

Work out which figure is a top-down 2D view of the 3D question figure.

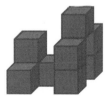

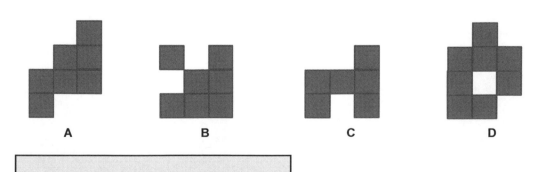

A   B   C   D

QUESTION 8

Work out which figure is a top-down 2D view of the 3D question figure.

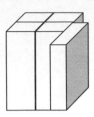

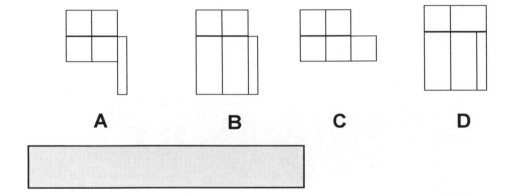

A   B   C   D

ANSWERS TO 2D VIEWS OF 3D SHAPES

Q1. D

- None of the answer options would show a 2D view of the 3D shape.

Q2. A

- A top-down 2D view of the 3D shape would show 7 squares, positioned like so:

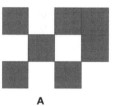

A

Q3. A

- A top-down 2D view of the 3D shape would show 11 squares, positioned like so:

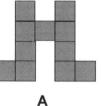

A

Q4. C

- A top-down 2D view of the 3D shape would show 6 squares, positioned like so:

C

Q5. A

- A top-down 2D view of the 3D shape would show 3 squares, positioned like so:

A

Q6. D

- A top-down 2D view of the 3D shape would only show 5 squares, positioned like so:

D

Q7. C

- A top-down 2D view of the 3D shape would show 6 squares, positioned like so:

C

Q8. A

- A top-down 2D view of the 3D shape would show 4 squares and one rectangle, positioned like so:

A

CUBES AND NETS

For these types of question, you need to be able to build the cube net in your head and work out where the shapes would be positioned on the cube.

<u>Let's take a look at a quick example:</u>

Work out which of the cubes can be made from the net.

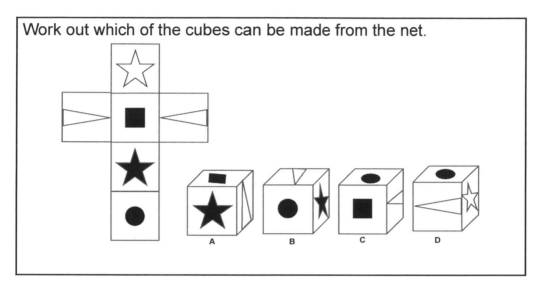

ANSWER = A

For these types of questions, you need to imagine that you are building a cube. The cube net has shapes on, so folding down the creases in order to make the cube, you need to work out where the shapes will be positioned. (Please note: these questions require you to fold the net so the shapes remain on the outside of the cube).

> Useful Practice Tip:
> Build your own paper cube and draw the shapes on it.
>
> Fold the cube to see where the shapes will be positioned.

The answer to the example above is A. If the star is positioned on the front of the cube, this means that either the square or the circle can be placed on top of the cube. Answer A works because if the star is facing the front and has the square at the top of the cube, the triangular shape will need to be positioned pointing upwards.

DAY 7 ➡ **Cubes and Nets**

Question Time!

QUESTION 1

Work out which of the cubes can be made from the net.

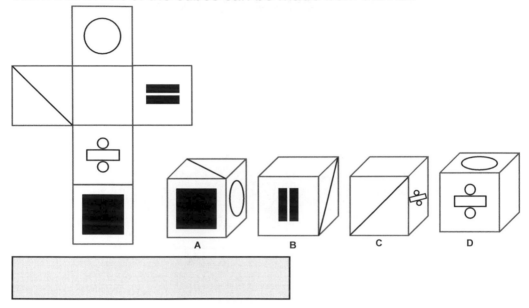

QUESTION 2

Work out which of the cubes can be made from the net.

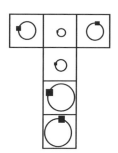   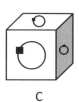 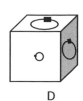

A   B   C   D

QUESTION 3

Work out which of the cubes can be made from the net.

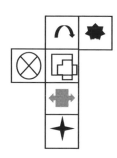 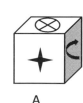 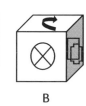 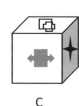 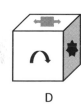

A   B   C   D

QUESTION 4

Work out which of the cubes can be made from the net.

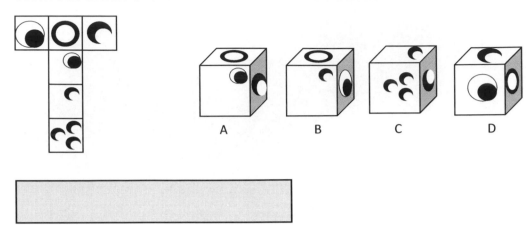

QUESTION 5

Work out which **TWO** cubes can be made from the net.

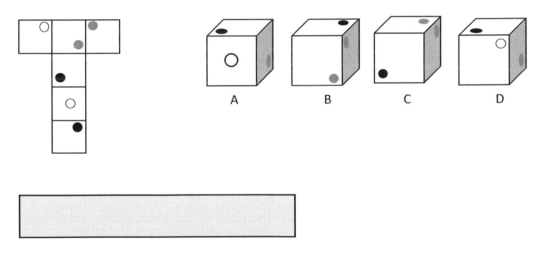

QUESTION 6

Work out which **TWO** cubes can be made from the net.

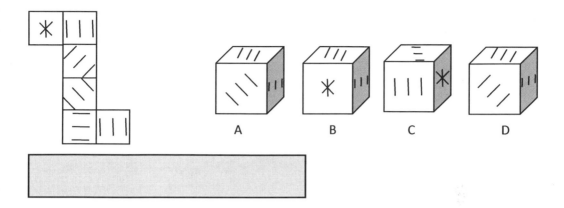

QUESTION 7

Work out which of the cubes can be made from the net.

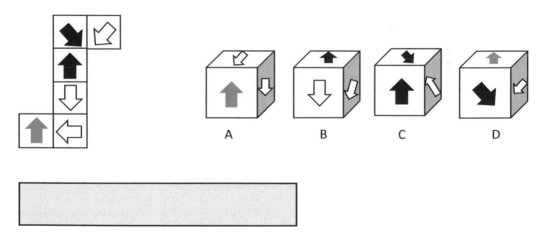

QUESTION 8

Work out which of the cubes can be made from the net.

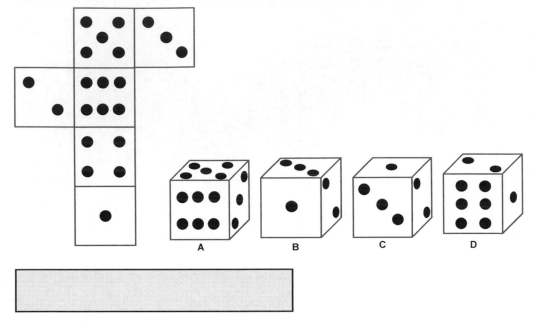

ANSWERS TO CUBES AND NETS

Q1. C

- Figure C is the correct answer. In order to work out where the shapes would be positioned, draw out a cube net (as shown in the question). Fold the cube net, and see what cube you end up with.

Q2. D

- Figure D is the correct answer. In order to work out where the shapes would be positioned, draw out a cube net (as shown in the question). Fold the cube net, and see what cube you end up with.

Q3. B

- Figure B is the correct answer. In order to work out where the shapes would be positioned, draw out a cube net (as shown in the question). Fold the cube net, and see what cube you end up with.

Q4. C

- Figure C is the correct answer. In order to work out where the shapes would be positioned, draw out a cube net (as shown in the question). Fold the cube net, and see what cube you end up with.

Q5. A and B

- Figure A and B are the correct answers. In order to work out where the shapes would be positioned, draw out a cube net (as shown in the question). Fold the cube net, and see what cube you end up with.

Q6. B and D

- Figure B and D are the correct answer. In order to work out where the shapes would be positioned, draw out a cube net (as shown in the question). Fold the cube net, and see what cube you end up with.

Q7. C

- Figure C is the correct answer. In order to work out where the shapes would be positioned, draw out a cube net (as shown in the question). Fold the cube net, and see what cube you end up with.

Q8. A

- Figure A is the correct answer. In order to work out where the shapes would be positioned, draw out a cube net (as shown in the question). Fold the cube net, and see what cube you end up with.

Day 7 Checklist

You have now completed your Day 7 revision.

How confident are you feeling?

Below we have included a checklist that you can tick off to make sure that you have learnt everything regarding this chapter.

I have read and understood the examples for tackling 2D Views of 3D Shapes questions.

I have read and understood the examples for tackling Cubes and Nets questions.

I have read and understood the top tips provided for my Day 7 revision.

I have read and understood the detailed answers and explanations to each question.

I feel confident in 2D Views of 3D Shapes questions.

I feel confident in Cubes and Nets questions.

IMPROVE YOUR 11+ ABILITY

Our How2Become 11+ revision guides are the ULTIMATE revision resources to prepare you fully for your 11+.

FOR MORE INFORMATION ON OUR 11+ GUIDES, PLEASE CHECK OUT THE FOLLOWING:

WWW.HOW2BECOME.COM

Get Access To

FREE

11+

TEST QUESTIONS

www.MyEducationalTests.co.uk

17646393R00096

Printed in Great Britain
by Amazon